LONELY EAGLES

THE STORY OF AMERICA'S BLACK AIR FORCE IN WORLD WAR II

By Robert A. Rose D.D.S.

Tuskegee Airmen Inc., Los Angeles Chapter

FIRST PRINTING AUGUST 1976
SECOND PRINTING MARCH 1980
THIRD PRINTING DECEMBER 1982
FOURTH PRINTING MAY 1988

Published By:
Tuskegee Airmen Inc., Los Angeles Chapter
3933 Sixth Avenue
Los Angeles, CA 90008

Library of Congress Catalog Card Number 76-28835

ISBN Number 0-917612-00-0 — Hardbound
ISBN Number 0-917612-01-9 — Softbound

DEDICATION

This effort is dedicated to all, living and dead, who shared in one of the most unique phases of the military history of the United States, the Tuskegee experience.

LONELY EAGLES is in no way intended as a definitive history of the Tuskegee story. Volumes could be written on the subject, however, to date, no one has. . . The names, places and incidents included are as historically accurate as research could provide. The selection of material is no more or less significant than that which has been excluded, but merely serves as examples which may hopefully answer questions regarding the controversy, misunderstanding and gross inaccuracies surrounding the role of the black person in the days of the segregated U.S. Army Air Forces.

Preface

A doctrine established in 1896 that Negroes were afforded equal rights as long as separate but equal facilities existed for separation of the races was not challenged by the Supreme Court until nine years after World War II. In the Army during this era, the separate but equal status of Negroes called for segregation into separate units, but the Army Air Corps did not until a Congressional Act in 1939 provide training units for Negro personnel.

Men of the first, and perhaps the best known of all Negro combat units, the 99th Fighter Squadron, had been carefully selected for the unit early in 1941. Each enlisted man had college training and a mechanical background. Candidates for training as commissioned pilots were selected in the same manner as prescribed for white candidates, with, however, a quota system to limit the number. After the completion of all phases of training in 1943, the 99th was sent to the Mediterranean Theater of Operations to operate with, but not a part of the 33rd, and later the 79th Fighter Group. While the 99th was receiving its baptism under fire, three other all Negro squadrons were being trained. Joining the 99th FS in Italy in 1944 they collectively became known as the 332nd Fighter Group and were assigned to the 12th & 15th Air Forces. All pilots of the "Negro Air Force" had been trained at Tuskegee, Alabama Army Air Field, where later, a Negro bomber group, the 477th was initiated.

In noting the rather conservative "art" seen in many of the accompanying photos, it must be realized that no personnel in any of the squadrons, including the commander, had ever been subjected to any perils, traditions or fads of military life in a combat zone. The desire to prove themselves as quality fighting men, little time was left for the frivolity of the more flamboyant characterizations seen on most aircraft during the war. Until the latter days of the war, art was limited to mothers, wives and girlfriends names or in the case of one pilot, all three; the order of which was reversed on two different aircraft flown by him during different periods. His preference at the time was probably based upon which one occupied most of his thoughts at the time the crew chief manned the paint brush. Grace-Marie-Rose, in bright red on a P-39, became Rose-Marie-Grace on a P-51. A P-40 in 1944 was conservatively inscribed "Wilma," but to a now seasoned veteran one year later adorned a mural like map of the entire state of New York, including major cities, on his aircraft now named "Wilma from White Plains." Cartoon characters such as "Daisy Mae," "Jiggs," and "Popeye," were rather popular, as everyone could identify with them. Also Negro slang of the era, such as "Goodwiggle," referring to an young lady while walking, whose anatomy either purposely, or otherwise was an attention getter. "Killer," meaning smooth and cool in behavior, "High Yellow," imploying light in complexion, and "Booty," a term applied to the intimate pleasures young men seek from young ladies. Such names as "Count," "Duke," or "Fatha" were nicknames of esteem and were frequently seen. The "A-Train," a New York subway leading to Harlem, "Central Avenue Breakdown" referring to the main street through the Negro district in Los Angeles, "125 & Lennox," the same reference to New York, were neatly and proudly inscribed.

A former C.O. of the 99th & 332nd, then Major George S. Roberts, the first black man to be selected for pilot training in the Air Corps, states that for quite some time the men were discouraged from naming or marking their P-40's with any symbol, name, or character which might identify the pilot. As it was, German intelligence had a complete dossier on the "Black Air Force," including the class records and reports kept at Tuskegee, and were estremely interested in the "Schwartze Vogelmenschen," and their new found place in aviation. It was felt that further identification was not necessary to aid the jerries.

It was very common practice to include the first name of a loved one of the pilot's choice, followed by the name of one close to his crew chief or other member of the squadron. In the case of Captain Wendell O. Pruitt of St. Louis, Mo., the hyphenated names of his fiancee and that of his crew chief resulted in the name "Alice-Jo." In nearly all cases the art was repeated on both port and starboard sides of the bird. Considering the fact that four types of aircraft were flown by the 332nd at one phase or another, the lids were off the paint cans regularly. The most identifying marking of the 332nd while flying Mustangs, was the all red tail surface, thus the nickname "Red Tails." Each of the four squadrons could be differentiated by the color of the trim tabs, the 99th being white, the 100th black, the 301st and 302nd being blue and yellow respectively. Also each squadron sported an identifying nose band just aft of the spinner; the 99th being blue and white checkerboard, the 100th, solid red, the 302nd alternate yellow and red horizontal stripes, and the 301st is believed to have been blue and red. The 99th was further identified by the letter "A" in conjunction with the aircraft number. All squadrons had red spinners, with certain variations as noted above, as did the other three Mustang Fighter Groups of the 15th Air Force. The Group also for a period of one month (June 44) flew "Jugs." The initial batch being razorback P-47 D's, all of which were handed down to them from the 325th "Checkertail Clan," who had already switched to P-51's. The markings of the 332nd at this time were not characteristic to the group, as they were not in this aircraft long enough to completely identify with them. In some, but not all cases, red tails were painted on them as they stood on the revetments between missions. As reported by Capt. Richard Caesar, the Engineering Officer, of the 100th, "Man, those jobs were tired and worn when we got them. We painted over the checkerboards in a hurry, some of the guys taking off with wet paint, and it wasn't until just before we were phased into the Mustangs, that a few natural metal bubble canopied Thunderbolts began to be ferried in from North Africa. We had time to group mark them properly then they were ditched when the Mustang arrived."

The foregoing has been a brief description of one of the most uniquely different groups in the USAAF in World War II. Its purpose is to acquaint readers with them and is the prelude to the story.

Table of Contents

COVER — The cover design denotes the emblem of Tuskegee Airmen, Inc. This logo, accepted as the national symbol was designed by: Robert A. Rose, D.D.S., and Oscar York, both of Tuskegee Airmen Inc., Los Angeles Chapter.

The Early Days
& The Birth of The 99th

Black airmen in World War II destroyed or damaged 409 enemy aircraft, including the last four victories of The Army Air Corps in the Mediterranean Theater of Operations. They flew 15,553 sorties, and 1578 missions. 200 of these missions were as heavy bomber escorts deep into the Rhineland, during which time, not one of the heavies was lost to enemy fighter opposition. They flew four types of first line fighter aircraft while in combat, and shot down three of a total of eight Messerschmitt 262 jets confirmed by the Fifteenth Air Force, 450 Negro pilots of the 99th, 100th, 301st, and 302nd Fighter Squadrons, known collectively as the 332nd Fighter Group distinguished themselves, culminating in a Presidential Unit Citation on March 24, 1945, reading in part: "Displaying outstanding courage, aggressiveness, and combat technique, the 332nd Fighter Group reflected great credit on itself and the armed forces of the United States of America..."

From the years 1932 to 1941, there were nine Negro aviators who had earned commercial pilots certificates under the Civil Aeronautics Administration. There were 102 licensed private pilots, and 160 licensed solo student pilots. In 1939, two of these flyers, Dale L. White, and Chauncey E. Spencer, with the sanction of the National Airmen's Association of America , and also with the political blessings of Governor Dwight Green, and Senator Everett M. Dirkson, both of Illinois, arranged for a cross country flight between Chicago and Washington, D.C. The purpose was to appeal through publicity to the U.S. Government, that as American citizens, Negroes should be included in government financed aviation training programs. Hopefully political pressures would open doors. The NAAA made efforts locally to raise money to finance the flight, but the answer in all instances was disappointing. The general consensus was that such a mission was ridiculous and foolhardy. The two pilots finally used their own money to rent an ancient Lincoln-Paige biplane, and were loaned

9

$1,000 by the Jones brothers in Chicago who headed a number-policy racket in that city. The flight was on.

Spencer and White flew from Harlem Airport, in Oaklawn, Illinois, as planned on May 9, 1939. Three hours later they were grounded in a farmer's back yard in Sherwood, Ohio, with a broken crankshaft. After two-and-one half days, they resumed their mission, and later were grounded in Pittsburgh for a night landing without lights behind a commercial airliner at the Allegheny Airport. However, the next morning the CAA cleared them to resume their flight, but they were forced to return to Pittsburgh because the Morgantown, West Virginia Airport was under construction and there was no place to store their plane. Upon learning of their plight, Mr. Robert L. Vann, the publisher of the Pittsburgh Courier, a black owned newspaper gave them $500 and letters of introduction to influential representatives in Washington. Upon their arrival in the capital, they had conferences with officials who promised support. It was on the electric car running underground to the Congressional building, that Mr. Edgar Brown, a member of the Negro press in Washington, introduced them to a man who probably did more to turn the tide toward the future of blacks in aviation than any other man or incidient up to that time.

The man introduced was Senator Harry S. Truman, of Missouri. Mr. Truman showed immediate surprise that Negroes were not included in the proposed training program soon to be inaugurated by the government, and a greater surprise that the Air Corps did not permit Negroes to enlist. After quite a lengthy discussion, and some time spent at the airport with the flyers, Mr. Truman said to Spencer and White: "If you guys had the guts to fly this thing to Washington, I've got the guts enough to see that you get what you are asking!" True to his word, Senator Truman directed his efforts to President Franklin D. Roosevelt, and Secretary of War Robert H. Hinckly, also to Congressman Arthur W. Mitchell, J. Hamilton Lewis, Everett M. Dirkson, and the Negro press. As a consequence, in 1939, Congressional action enabled Negroes to enter civilian flight training. Two laws, based upon the separate but equal policy were enacted.

One was the Civilian Pilot Training Act Program (CPTP), which was administered by the Civil Aeronautics Autority (CAA), and authorized certain colleges and universities to instruct students to fly. The purpose of the program was to build a backlog of civilian pilots who could quickly be adapted to military aviation in the event of a national emergency. At the time the program was initiated, only eight Negro pilots held commercial ratings and since the law stated that no one could be denied training on account of race, creed, or color, the future appeared considerably brighter.

Six Negro colleges were selected as active participants in the CPTP program, these being: Howard University, Delaware State College, Hampton Institute, North Carolina A & T, West Virginia State College, and Tuskegee Institute. All of these facilities however, were in the south, and though the greater concentration of Negro students was in this area, many northern residents were geographically eliminated. In some isolated cases, one or two Negroes were trained in white CPTP schools. As a result, two Negro non-college units in the Chicago area were formed, one of them by Miss Willa B. Brown, who was among the first commercially licensed Negro fliers. Miss Brown owned and operated The Coffey School of Aeronautics, named for her late husband Cornelius Coffey, one of the first black men in the country to hold both a certified instructors license, as well as an airplane and engine mechanics certificate. The dynamic and energetic Miss Brown had previously been very instrumental in the organization of the NAAA, and promotion of the cross county flight of Spencer and White. The Coffey School, located at The Harlem Airport, offered the full range of CPTP and War Training Services, and was the hub of the Negro Civil Air Patrol acitivity when that program was instituted in 1941.

The second law, passed concurrently with the CPTP act, was Public Law 18. It stated that the Air Corps needed additional training facilities for its primary training, and that the U.S. Government would stock and supply the civilian schools, monitor and dispatch the necessary funds to see that prescribed military standards were upheld. As the existing schools delivering the CPTP program were also the facilities to receive government funds, including the Negro schools, it was assumed that some of the personnel being trained would be acceptable candidates for cadet training in the Army Air Corps . As it turned out, this was partially true, but only after months of debate and government evasion of the issue. The general public also had the mistaken impression that a connection now existed between the CAA program and the opening of the Air Corps to Negroes in the various phases of training. However, the actual participation of Negroes in the CPTP program did not allay the agitation for full participation in the Air Corps as was hoped by the War Department, but only kindled the fires already burning, and gave further leverage to the campaign. Further fuel was added to the fire when the second school in the Chicago area, located at Glenview, and specifically set up for the purpose of training Negroes, failed to admit any, though the facilities were prepared for them. This encouraged the War Department to provide a standard answer: "We are having difficulty in finding twenty qualified students needed to begin instruction and now that the War Department is funding and financing the program, and it is the policy not to mix colored and white men in the same tactical organization, and since no provision has been made for any colored Air Corps units in the Army, colored persons are not eligible for enlistment in the Air Corps, so there is no need for additional facilities." As a result, white cadet classes were being sent there.

During the first year of the CPTP, 100 Negro college students were given training; of these 91 qualified for civil licenses, a record, according to a national magazine, as good as that of white students. Tuskegee Institute was given prime status in 1940, as it was the largest of the Negro programs, and though it was necessary to utilize a commercial airport some 40 miles away in Montgomery, it was one of a few educational institutions to provide both flying and ground instruction at that time. Through the dedication and determination of two men, Dr. Fred L. Patterson, President of Tuskegee Institute, and Mr. George L. Washington, Director of Mechanical Industries at the school, a lease was secured on a tract of land some five miles from the institute. With an alumni drive, contributions, student help, and their own hard labor, Kennedy Field, or Airport No. 1, was completed. However, so rapid was the increase in the program size, that the secondary students had to use the field at Alabama Polytechnic College, some 20 miles away, nearly as unsuitable as the Montgomery arrangement.

As the battle over the interpretation of Public Law 18 continued, with such proponents as Senator Styles Bridges, Republican from New Hampshire, leading the way and gaining more strength in his argument that, "I find the provision of the law has not been carried out. Congress passed in good faith, a law to provide Air Corps training for the colored men of this country who desire to participate. To date it is evident that this law has been ignored!"

Finally by passing the Selective Service Act of 1940, which required all branches of the service to enlist Negroes, with no discrimination regarding race, color or creeed, the argument appeared settled, but for weeks, the Air Corps found flaws in all suggestions made for the beginning of training. G-3 suggested The Chicago School of Aeronautics give flying training, "but since mechanic training was not given here, it could not be used, for after all, if we have Negro pilots, we have to have Negro mechanics to service the planes." The Aeronautical University of Chicago gave mechanic training, but its students were housed in a YMCA, "which makes it impossible to assign colored students under the existing arrangement of racial separation. Housing, messing, concurrent civilian and military classes would make such assignments impossible."

It was therefore decided in favor of the Air Corps Technical School at Chanute Field, Illinois, where the Negroes and their facilities would be completely under military control. The Air Plans Division, on the other hand was certain that if this arrangement were made, "disturbances and riots will probably ensue both at the field, and within the nearby communities." As an alternative, Tuskegee Institute was suggested as the place to initiate such a course, so as to coordinate the service schools and pilot training. The Training and Operation Division held out for Chanute Field as the path of least resistance, because "such a small number of Negroes are expected anyway in view of the lack of qualified instructors, supervisors, and equipment."

In October 1940, The War Department stated that Negroes were in training as pilots, mechanics, and technical specialists, but Judge William H. Hastie, Civilian Aide on Negro Affairs to the Secretary of War, repudiated the announcement, and related that civil flying instruction at a few Negro colleges, and The Coffey School, all under the jurisdiction of the CAA, was still the only training available to Negroes. Finally after eliminating California and Texas as possible training facilities, and the War Department admitting it had been a little premature in its announcement regarding its program in training Negro flyers, Tuskegee Institute was selected as the location of choice for pilot training for the United States Army Air Corps, with Chanute Field assigned the contract for training mechanics, and auxilliary personnel.

In December of 1940, the Air Corps presented its plan for the utilization of Negroes. This called for the employment of enlisted men and officers in a pursuit squadron, a base group detachment, weather and communications detachments, and the many and varied allied services necessary to establish a "separate Air Corps." White commissioned and noncommissioned officers, all on a voluntary basis, were to be used as instructors, inspectors, and supervisors for the period of time necessary to train and replace them with qualified Negro personnel. General Henry H. Arnold claimed however, that a period of three years would be necessary to train a crew chief, two more years for a hangar chief, and total of ten years for a line chief. He felt therefore, that a Negro combat unit could never be formed in time to be of value, if at all, to our national defense. In spite of General Arnold's pessimism, the plan proceeded, with the final determination that only basic and advanced stages would be instructed, as the elementary phase would be initiated by utilizing the Negro graduates from the CAA's civilian pilot training. This plan was supplemented in the spring of 1941 by authorization of a civil contract for elementary flight training of Negro cadets at Tuskegee.

Plans at Tuskegee Institute were rapidly proceeding, and Airport No. 2, or Moton Field, about four miles from the original Kennedy Field (Airport No. 1), was being completed with money borrowed from The Julius Rosenwald Fund. This was made possible through the help of Mrs. Eleanor Roosevelt, a member of

The Board of Trustees, and a vigorous fighter for civil rights long before it became popular to do so. This field was restricted to Army primary training of all Negro cadets, with the institute providing the civilian instructors, equipment, and facilities at government expense, including six nearly new Stearman PT-13A Kaydets.

The first flying cadets were inducted into the Army flying school and began primary training on July 19, 1941, and during this same period of time, Dr. Patterson of Tuskegee Institute received official word from the Assistant Secretary of War, that $1,091,000 (final cost $4,000,000) had been appropriated for the construction of Tuskegee Army Air Field, (Airport No. 3) where the cadets would receive their basic and advanced training, combat techniques, and finally receive their wings and commissions. Initial plans called for the 99th Pursuit Squadron, consisting of 400 officers and enlisted men, 33 pilots, and 33 planes. At the base would be constructed hangars, repair shops, classroom and laboratory facilities, administrative facilites, flight surgeon and infirmary areas, a dining hall, fire house, dormitories, and the many necessities to render the base completely functional and self sustaining. A dream had apparently come true.

Mr. Charles Alfred Anderson, of Bryn Mawr, Pennsylvania, was selected as the chief civilian flight instructor at Moton Field, which had opened August 23, 1941. Mr. Anderson had come to Tuskegee in July 1940 to teach the first advanced (secondary) course under The Civilian Pilot Training Program. "Chief" Anderson, as he was to become affectionately known, had acquired his commercial license in 1932, and had over 3,500 hours prior to accepting his appointment as primary chief instructor. Three other Negro instructors, Charles R. Foxx, Milton P. Crenshaw, and Sherman T. Rose, formed the backbone of the primary school, and were CPTP advanced training course graduates, and graduates of the instructors course, as was Mr. Anderson. Other primary pioneers include: Wendell R. Lipscomb, Adolph J. Moret, Perry Young, Claude R. Platt, and Charles Foreman, to mention a few. The initial commanding officer of primary training was Captain Noel F. Parrish. It was he who had, in the summer of 1939, assisted in opening the Army Primary School at Glenview, Illinois, one of the original Army Civilian Contract Primary Schools, as described earlier. The Tuskegee, Alabama school, now known as the 66th Army Air Force Training Detachment, on December 1, 1941, came under the command of Lt. William T. Smith, Captain Parrish going on to assume duty as the Director of Training at the Tuskegee Army Air Base. It may be interesting to note that the primary school mechanics and auxiliary staff, as well as the instructors were all civilians, including a young black woman, Miss Marjorie Cheatham, a licensed and certified aviation mechanic.

14

In the meantime, the cadets were housed and fed on the campus of Tuskegee Institute, during the five weeks prior to the beginning of flight training. Twelve cadets, and one student officer reported for this preflight training. The student officer was a West Point graduate, Captain Benjamin O. Davis Jr., who proved invaluable in providing the first class with the proper fundamentals of military training. Captain Davis, a 1936 graduate of the U.S. Military Academy, and son of Brigadier General B. O. Davis Sr., the first black man to hold the rank of General in the United States Army, had entered the Air Corps after duty at Fort Benning, Georgia and Fort Riley, Kansas as an infantry officer. At the time, General, and Captain Davis were the only two Negro line officers in the U.S. Army, the other three officers being chaplains. The appointment of Davis was therefore a rather natural sequence of events, in that no other man possessed the experience in the military, the rank or the ability to assume the responsibility of leadership planned for him. Captain Davis completed his flight training, and became the first black man to officially solo an aircraft as an officer of the Army Air Corps. The date was September 2, 1941.

As in all primary schools, it was found that some students had the requisite ability and desire, while others did not. Those falling in the latter catagory were eliminated, and those who were able to meet the requirements continued in training. Percentages in the first class were not significantly different from the general average, Air Corps washouts at that time were 50-60% and the experienced Army personnel, who supervised the training, repeatedly emphasized the fact that these percentages had always varied considerably where small groups were involved. The members initially inducted into the Air Corps were supposedly selected on the same basis as were white pilots, but a definite quota system prevented many qualified men from being accepted for pilot training, and related services. In many cases, the waiting list and the period of time for induction was at times stretched to the point of being ridiculous, with the result being many were drafted into other branches while waiting. Also, some men were under the false impression that becoming members of the CPTP program at Tuskegee would in some way assure their acceptance for military training. This was not true, as the two programs were separate.

Running concurrently with the program for pilot training, was the Chanute Field Technical School for auxilliary personnel. Most noteworthy at this time was the selection of men to fill the openings for aviation mechanics. Their selection was similar to that for pilots, in that Negro colleges were used as the source of supply. Most noteworthy in this group were: Tuskegee Institute, Morehouse College in Atlanta, Hampton Institute in Virginia, North Carolina A&T, and Fisk University in Nashville, Tennessee. Students at these institutions were notified as to the plans for establishing an Air Corps unit for Negroes, and applications were submitted. At this time, no one was sure as to the ultimate goal the War Department had in mind for Negroes, and again there was confusion and misdirection of efforts.

One such student was McGary Edwards, of Elkins, West Virginia. Edwards was a student in Mechanical Engineering at Tuskegee in mid 1941. Mrs. Eleanor Roosevelt, while visiting the institute, told him and others of the proposed Air Corps program. Edwards, along with about thirty students made application. He recalls: "It was quite amazing to me to see the caliber of men being selected for induction. It must be remembered that none of these men were being selected for pilot training, yet their educational level, achievement exam scores, and general qualifications should have rendered them all as officer candidates. Many had already been refused pilot training, and hoped this avenue would later open the door to their real dream. This was not to be however, and some of the men had a very difficult time adjusting to their white supervisors, instructors, and officers, most of whom weren't nearly as qualified to teach, nor direct, as were the students."

Upon arriving at Chanute, Edwards recalls the confusion and lack of preparation for the Negro program. Class organization and instructor selection left a little to be desired, and initially, the men had considerable spare time. They soon became quite proficient at marching and close order drill, and shortly became the talk of Chanute Field, and Rantoul, Illinois. Their splendid formations, and outstanding routine so impressed the base commander, that it was rumored that he had plans to utilize them completely as a precision drill team to represent Chanute in the annual Army competition. After all, he really didn't believe the Army was serious about training all those black men as aviation mechanics, and skilled technicians.

Upon completion of their nine, and sometimes twelve month "separate but equal" training, the men were sent to Maxwell Field, Alabama to await assignment. As only one station was available to the men, it being the incompleted Tuskegee Army Air Field, it was necessary for all to remain at Maxwell, where there was nothing for them to do. Again, no preparation had been made for their stay at the field, and since the military wanted to take no chances upon allowing them to pollute the city of Montgomery, it was decided that they remain on the base without benefit of leave. Finally, after about three weeks, an executive order allowed men off-base priviliges until Tuskegee was ready for them.

The first twelve cadets (thirteen including Davis) were: John C. Anderson Jr., an all American from Toledo University, a sixteen letter man and a straight "A" student. All the students felt that if anyone was predestined to make it, Anderson was the one. This was not the case; he washed out. Next was Charles D. Brown, a graduate of Johnson C. Smith College, and former member of the 100th Coast Artillery, from Abbeville, South Carolina. He also dropped out during basic. Theodore Brown, who hailed from New York City, via Northwestern University, with a B.A. and M.A., being only one course short of a Ph.D., was an extremely articulate young man. This failed to win his wings. Fredrick H. Moore, the only graduate of Tuskegee Institute in this initial class was from Sommerville, New Jersey, and already licensed by the CAA. He too failed during advanced training. Ulysses S. Pannell, came from Regan, Texas. His alma mater was Prairie View College, gaining there a degree in agriculture. Many fellow students believed Pannell came into the service to gain knowledge at government expense, yet with no intention of remaining in the Air Corps. As surmised, when he felt he had enough, he washed himself out, and returned to his native Texas, using his newly acquired flying skills to benefit his agricultural vocation. At this time, there was no war, and no further military obligation existed, so that when a man failed his prescribed courses, he simply went home. Then there was Marion A. Carter, formerly of the 184th Field Artillery. He was from Chicago, and his former military experience enabled him to become cadet sergeant of the group. It was quite a day for the rest of the cadets, when he reported resplendent in boots, riding pants, spurs, complete with riding crop, and shiny Sam Brown belt. His military experience, sartorial elegance, and degree from Central YMCA College in Chicago was not enough, however, as he too was no longer around at graduation. William Slade of Raleigh, North Carolina, enlisted after obtaining his degree from Knoxville College. Rodrick Williams, from the windy city, with a A.B. degree from the University of Illinois, was also a CPTP graduate. Both of these men were eliminated during basic and advanced. The following four (along with Captain Davis) successfully completed their training: Lemuel R. Custis, a former policeman from Hartford, Connecticut, had a college degree from Howard University. Charles DeBow, a graduate from Hampton Institute in business administration, was from Indianapolis, Indiana and CAA graduate. Mac Ross, a native of Dayton, Ohio, graduate of West Virginia State College, also a CAA graduate, was an inspector in an iron works in Ohio, before enlisting. He was continually worried, although his mechanical skills as a pilot were superior, he realized he just didn't get along with books. Last was George Spencer "Spanky" Roberts, who too was a graduate of West Virginia State College, and a native of Fairmont, West Virginia. Spanky probably had more natural ability than any of the others. He was the type of person one would expect to succeed at anything he tried; he took pride in his ability at the controls of a plane. He enjoyed extra privileges extended to him by his primary instructor, Charles Foxx, with whom he had taken his CPTP training. Foxx would allow him to perform any maneuver he desired (when off by themselves), most of which were never tried even in advanced training, much less in a PT-13A. In fact, Mr. Foxx learned a little from the unauthorized flights himself, often wondering who was the instructor.

Roberts, the first Negro accepted the Air Corps for cadet training, always remembers his acceptance, and states that the man probably most responsible for his selection in the first class was Major Smith. Spanky recalls, "I don't even remember his first name, but if you can imagine in those days, the guy was a Major, and was the commandant of Maxwell Field, Alabama. While I was there, after passing my exams, and speaking to him about my future in the Air Corps, he told of cadets being offered a choice of three class groups, and locations for training. If by the time the third choice was given and the man had not made his decision, he would be dropped from the program. My first choice was Parks Air College, but Major Smith advised me to pass that up, as well as my second choice. His reasoning was, and how true it turned out to be, that even if accepted at these flying schools, there would be no way to complete training without being washed out under the existing policy of segregation. The major said that plans were in the making for a Negro base at Tuskegee, and by the time it would be completed, my third option would enable me to be stationed there."

Upon completion of their primary training in the nine week Air Corps schedule at that time, the students were to be transferred to the new TAAF center for their basic and advanced. There was the expected thrill of flying BT-13s and AT-6s, but due to a variety of problems, the new base was not ready. Having been assisted by Army advice and supervision, Tuskegree Institute secured 1,600 acres of land six and one half miles northeast of Tuskegee town, and construction began. The field when completed was to become one of the largest in the south, and was the first such project to be designed and built by Negro architects and contractors. However, by the time the first class was ready for its basic training, due to unexpected grading and construction difficulties, as well as weather, only one runway was ready for use. The cadets had another distinction in that they were the only class in the history of TAAF to have had their own "chauffeur and car." Because of construction, and mud, the road from the temporary housing to the flight line was never the same from day to day, and the complexity of the route made it necessary for "Pompy" Hawkins to drive the old Ford and the cadets over new ground both morning and afternoon of each flight day. All the guys loved Pompy, and they would make wagers as to which direction the good sergeant would take, and the time necessary to do so.   Despite this slight difficulty, flight training was continued without interruption, and the students became quite accustomed to cross wind landings. Luck, as well as skill and careful supervision, was with them in all phases of their training. The accident rate was very low, and throughout its period of training, the first class did not seriously damage a single aircraft. Initially, Tuskegee Army Air Field had been alloted six PT-13s, four BT-13s, and four AT-6s.

During this period of construction, Major James A. "Straight Arrow" Ellison assumed command of the new Field. Late in October 1941, the ground detachment arrived, having completed its training at Chanute Field, and its temporary confinement at Maxwell. The cadets now entering basic training would work with the ground crews. In January, Colonel Frederick V. Kimble replaced Major Ellison, and it was he who was responsible for the field becoming a functioning unit in spite of the local, national, and in some cases military adverse publicity, and sentiment over the whole project, not to mention the unavoidable construction problems. Major Ellison had done his job adequately in formulating the base, but it had been rumored that he fell into disfavor with local authorities for standing up for the rights of a Negro sentry at the base for challenging a white civilian, therefore leading to his transfer.

In spite of the many problems encountered in completing this new undertaking, not just negative forces prevailed. The War Department, due to excessive pressure was making an effort to establish a token working program. One must remember that times were different, and no project had been established as a guideline, so that trial, error and misunderstanding were all necessary in quest of an adequate solution. Throughout the existence of TAAF, the greater majority of cadets felt that the instructors were conscientious, having volunteered for duty at Tuskegee, insuring a degree of sincerity and fairness toward the students. When friction did develop, it was usually a result of orders from higher up, or from non-flying white staff and ground personnel of lower rank who were reluctant to accept the black cadets and officers. Three men who were directly responsible for the success or failure of each of the cadets during the early days at TAAF were: Captain Gabe C. Hawkins, Director of Basic Training, a true dyed-in-the-wool southerner, who impressed the men with one notable characteristic of a BT-13, if no other. His words of wisdom were, "in the event of engine failure, don't you boys never try a 180 degree turn because this BT will sail like a rock." He did, and nearly spread himself all over the Alabama countryside. By some miracle the medics put him back together. He remained in the Air Corps in a non-flying capacity.

Captain Robert M. Long, Director of Advanced Training, was lovingly called "Mother" by the cadets. He was so named because of his attaching so many of them to his apron strings, in hopes that the fittest would survive. Many denied any uncomplimentary connotation in his nickname, others disagree and imply no endearment in its application.

Major Donald G. McPherson, was Director of Fighter Training. If a cadet was requested to take to the air with "Black Barney", as he was not so lovingly called, the student was in trouble.

McPherson acquired this name because of his seemingly never clean shaven appearance. He wore a five o'clock shadow twenty four hours a day, and strongly resembled the villian in the Buck Rogers comic strip; hense his nickname. The men nearly unanimously compared his handling of an aircraft to the dexterity applied in driving a truck. Finesse and feeling were not part of his repertoire. All hated him in school, but appreciated his logic and wisdom after becoming fighter pilots.

The neighboring basic school, Gunter Field, in Montgomery, and the advanced school, at Maxwell Field, co-operated by allowing full use of their auxiliary fields, night flying facilities, and even planes, when these were required by the uncompleted Tuskegee school. Gunnery training for the TAAF base was performed at the Air Corps Gunnery School at Eglin Field, Florida, and though individual problems occurred with a fair amount of frequency, self restraint, and level headedness prevented the type of incidents so many had predicted. A few hot heads exchanged words, and blows, and every now and again, an irate farmer would take a shot at a low flying airplane. Whether the "buzzing" of his farm and field hands by "them pesky Tuskegee niggers" came before, or after the pot shots at the aircraft was not known, but in any event no record of injury or worse was known to have come of it.

The failure of eight of the initial class of thirteen to graduate, brought feelings of bitter disappointment in many cases, resulting, no doubt, from the fact that the cadets were aware and conscious of the unusual amount of attention they were attracting, and their intense desire to prove themselves. This also caused additional stress on the cadets who were successful. It was probably difficult enough to fly, without feeling that 13,000,000 black Americans were depending upon them as a source of inspiration. The dangers inherent in too much interest and attention were recognized very early by the Air Corps, as many felt and often expressed that these cadets should be expected to fly in some manner different from other airmen. The fact that they were Negroes was incidental and no strange and peculiar traits should come from that. Flying was still flying, and aside from any social problems which occurred, the airplane reacted the same to black or white hands. The facts seem quite obvious, but it was surprising the thousands of otherwise well informed people, both black and white, who showed a tendency to think irrationally when they thought of the Negro aviators.

Shortly after his graduation, then 2nd Lieutenant Charles DeBow, published in The American Magazine, August 1942, some of his feelings regarding his new role as a black man in the Air Corps. Lieutenant DeBow remembers a white civilian on the street in Montgomery one day asking: "You one of those new colored fliers over at Tuskegee?" "Yes sir," DeBow proudly replied. "Tell me one thing. What do you boys want to fly for, anyhow?" DeBow really couldn't think of an adequate answer at the time, but upon thinking it over afterward, said his own mind was sufficiently clear to realize that he was flying for his country. He felt that however imperfect our democracy was, its the only system which could open the way to perfection, and he wanted no part of a Fascist future. He recalled thinking, he was flying for his mother and dad, who struggled in menial labor to provide an opportunity for him. He felt he had a job to do for his country, and his race, and just as Booker T. Washington and George Washington Carver proved themselves as educator and scientist, he might prove to someone that Negroes could become good pilots and officers. Lieutenant DeBow summed up rather nicely what probably went through the minds of all of his classmates as their wings were pinned on them that morning of March 7, 1942.

Lieutenant Mac Ross, a classmate of Charles DeBow was so concerned with succeeding, that shortly after graduation, an incident occurred that made him believe he may have shattered the entire program, and it further exemplified the added pressures on the young aviators. It happened during the early stages of fighter transitional training, while flying a P-40F, along with Lieutenants DeBow, Custis, and Roberts. While in tight formation someone noticed smoke pouring from Ross' engine cowling. Flying at 6,000 feet, wing tips but feet apart, they loosened the formation. Mac fought to bring the 40 home. Finally after much persuasion by his mates, at 3,000 feet, he bailed out, and landed safely in a cotton field. For days, although completely cleared of pilot error, Ross' only thought was, "I've wrecked a ship worth thousands of dollars. Maybe they'll start saying that Negroes can't fly after all!" He therefore had the rather dubious distinction of being the first Negro to survive the loss of a military plane in flight, becoming the first colored member of the "Caterpillar Club."

Even though steady progress was made at the field, the War Department was reluctant about increasing the quota of cadets admitted for training. By the time the first class, 42-C, had graduated, two other classes were in training, getting their wings at four-and-one-half week intervals. Those graduating in class 42-D, were: Sidney Brooks, Charles W. Dryden, and Clarence C.

Jamison. Class 42-E, or No. 3 graduates being: James B. Knighten, George L. Knox, Lee Rayford, and Sherman W. White. To this point, and for many classes to come, restriction limited class size to no more than ten, the token quota established by the War Department.

In the meantime, the overall war effort was continuing. Training bases for pilots and auxiliary personnel, and the output of thousands of new airplanes occupied much of the headline news. Conscientious young men from all walks of life were becoming involved. Such was George Haley, who dropped out of Syracuse University in the fall of 1942 "because they were screaming for pilots" and he wanted to do his part. He passed the Army Air Corps pilot training test and was sent home to Bath, New York to "await" call up. Although it was the height of World War II, he waited nearly a year, much to the concern of the local draft board, and the neighboring families whose own sons had been quickly swept off to battle. "They had a quota of 52 pilots a year. That's all they allotted for Tuskegee at that time," remarked Haley.

Herman "Ace" Lawson, formerly of the 99th, and later a city councilman in Sacramento, California, recalls the runaround he received upon application for pilot training. He learned to fly initially in gliders, and while at Fresno State College, as the only black in a class of twenty in the CPTP program, received his pilots license. After seeing an advertisement that the Air Corps examining board would be interviewing students, Lawson joined his buddies, who were going down to sign up. After standing in line for nearly an hour for his interview, he came face to face with a white major, who bluntly questioned his presence in line. Lawson said he'd never forget the look in the major's eyes when he was told, "Get the hell out of here boy, the Army isn't training night fighters!" Unfortunately, Lawson was not aware that the laws of his country which established segregation, also prohibited him from joining the Air Corps. Finally after some period of time and much frustration, the word came that Negroes would be accepted, and "Ace" applied. He recalls waiting five more months, with no word. He wrote his congressman, senator and even President Roosevelt. Finally after two more months, he received word to report for duty, and was accepted for aviation cadet training. At the time he was a school photographer at Fresno State College, with about $1,000 worth of camera equipment stored in the trunk of his 1935 Pylmouth convertible. So eager was he to report that he left equipment and Plymouth sitting at the railroad depot, and departed for March Field for induction before the Air Corps changed its mind. To this day, he has seen neither equipment, nor car.

The NAACP had requested that Negro cadets be accepted and

trained on the basis of fitness, without regard to a ten per cent racial quota, on which the government was alleged to have made its selection, though actually, it was less than that. Also, Mr. Langston H. Caldwell, chairman of Tuskegee Airmen Association called attention to the fact that over 100 private pilots trained at Tuskegree had filed application to become cadets, but only two had been called to that date. By the time class 42-K had graduated in December, the allocation for cadet training had increased, and the beginning of 1943 showed a marked increase, due to plans to expand the squadron into a group.

On December 26, 1942, the now Lieutenant Colonel Noel F. Parrish had assumed command of Tuskegee Army Air Field. Colonel Kimble had aroused considerable resentment for his catering to local racist policies, and for having no real feeling of the problems surrounding Negroes. Though Colonel Parrish made no immediate substantial changes at Tuskegee, his understanding and patience contributed to a more successful administration. He developed a keen interest, and sense of awareness of the effect of traditional southern practices on Negroes, and was able to follow through on his assignment with much more tact and diplomacy. He met with, and talked with Negro leaders, read extensively of racist problems prevalent at the base upon his arrival, as well as the problems created by segregation throughout the country in general, and gained much respect on all fronts for his fair minded thinking.

The War Department broke its long silence concerning plans for the utilization of the 99th. It announced that it expected the squadron would very soon be sent for overseas duty. This action, however, stimulated no feelings of optimism, as it was not the first time the men had been alerted for possible combat action. The War Department had originally programmed the Tuskegee men for movement overseas in the Liberia Task Force movement. During the months that followed this announcement, the troops had been in various stages of alert. They had seen certain units of the task force disbanded due to cancellation of the original orders, and were not certain the same thing would not happen to them. The men of the 99th Fighter Squadron, 83rd Fighter Control Squadron, and 689th Signal Air Warning Company had finished their training, and were literally worn out with combat refresher training. They became known as "Lonely Eagles," destined to fly alone, if at all. No furloughs were possible, and often pass privileges were withdrawn when immediate movement communications, which did not result in movement orders, were received. Mental strain and tension mounted as the fear that "something" might happen to prevent their use in combat. That the squadron might dry rot before ever getting overseas was a major concern of the men during the months of waiting. Concern about the speed of shipment of white units and pilots with less training time by the Negro press did little to increase the morale of the men. The War Department felt that perhaps every effort should be made to move the troops to some other locality, preferably in the direction of their ultimate destination. They felt the mere activity of moving would satisfy them for a reasonable length of time, and strange surroundings would quiet their restlessness. The problem here being, where were they going to send all those Negroes?

It was over this issue, as well as how the training of existing units was carried out, failure to expand the units at the rate originally scheduled by the War Department, and failure to place qualified Negro officers as department heads, even when of higher rank than their white contemporaries who held the positions, that tendered the resignation of Judge William H. Hastie, Civilian Aide on Negro Affairs to The Secretary of War. Judge Hastie had been instrumental previously on his stand regarding Negroes and the CPTP program. Failure to extend to Negroes the benefit of training available to white personnel, as well as the perpetuation of overt segregation became so objectionable and inexcusable, that Judge Hastie felt his presence no longer useful. Hastie's resignation was to take effect on January 31, 1943, and was directly preceded and followed by certain immediate changes in the Air Corps. A description of the changes brought about is in order.

Tuskegee Army Air Field, had now grown to a total of 217 officers, and 3,000 enlisted men. The War Department still emphasized the fact that Negro officers were not placed in positions of responsibility, because they were not yet qualified, and that the efficiency of the unit would be reduced if these positions were filled with unqualified men. What was really true, was that no arrangements were being made to qualify the able and competent Negroes. The prospect that Tuskegee would become an all-Negro post, as specified in its initial conception, was not bright. But consistant with the goal of training the Negro personnel with the least difficulty, the Air Corps continued to add training facilities at Tuskegee, thereby relieving itself of the necessity of training Negro specialists and technicians at its established schools, and at the same time severely burdening the entire training program being administered there. Judge Hastie protested and objected to the expensive and uneconomical utilization of personnel and material to duplicate training for so small a number of men compared to the total Air Corps picture. Finally in August 1942. the Air Corps Technical Training Command admitted that the facilites at Tuskegee were no longer able to keep pace with the enlargement of the program. Therefore, whether desired or not, the program was enlarging itself. The War Department had planned on establishing Jefferson Barracks, in St. Louis, Missouri, as the Negro Officers Training School, but again, the good judge brought pressure on the Secretary of War's office, and emphasized that such establishment would but further perpetuate the expenses of duplicate training facilities. The plans for carrying out this measure were quietly dropped, as were proposals for all future segregated bases. It was decided that Lincoln, Nebraska, and Tuskegee AAF concentrate on training mechanics, with Buckley Field, Lowry Field, Fort Logan, and Grand Rapids, function as bases for various technical specialties. Harvard and Yale Universities were also considered for communications, engineering, armament, and statistical courses. Though being trained separately from the white personnel, progress had been made in that both black and white were now located, in most cases, and carrying on similar duties on the same base.

It could not be denied that the program of pilot training was proving successful, and the caliber of men being turned out was on a par with Air Corps standards. It became apparent that replacements pilots would be necessary, as well as the auxiliary staff previously discussed. On the 19th of February, 1942, a second squadron was approved. This was the 100th Fighter Squadron. Again it was Judge Hastie who made the most skeptical realize that the program at Tuskegee was unable to handle the rapid growth, and on May 26th of the same year, the squadron was activated, with plans for its removal to new yet undetermined quarters. In the meantime the 100th was to remain at Tuskegee, and soon become the cadre for the contemplated 332nd Fighter Group.

While many of the Air Corps proposals were not carried out, plans for a medium bombardment group were initiated, and did materialize (the 477th Bomb Group, Medium), and Flight Surgeons were ordered to school at Randolph Field, Texas, whereas before, the Negro medical men were forced to take their training in aviation medicine through correspondence courses.

By February, 1943, it had become apparent to all at Tuskegee that the North African Theater was selected as the destination of the 99th, and that definite plans were made for its entry into combat. Plans for the 99th to join General Claire Chennault's forces in China were considered, but it was generally felt that sending an inexperienced squadron into this zone would result in such heavy losses as to be politically dangerous.

The pilots and ground crews were given even more intensive training in combat tactics, in their P-40s, and were told to grasp every bit of knowledge they could, they'd need it. The squadron for its proficiency received commendations throughout the Southeast Training Command. Their formation flying was not again performed with such precision and regularity until the formation of Air Force flight demonstration teams years later. The ground crews were exceptionally sharp, performing engine changes in one third the time normally required. The optimism and comaraderie was at a peak, and the original squadron leader, now Captain George S. Roberts, was replaced by now Lieutenant Colonel Benjamin O. Davis, Jr. The "old man" as Davis was known by his junior officers, had been promoted from Captain to Lieutenant Colonel in two and one half weeks, in order to reach the level already attained by his contemporaries as determined by the Air Corps promotion board. Davis' promotions were so rapid that he never wore majors oakleaves. He therefore named his dog "Major." During this period, Colonel Davis was being groomed for the position of commander and had it not been for rank, Captain Roberts, who was doing a splendid job, with the respect of his fellow flying officers, and the enlisted men as well, would have remained as C.O. As it was, he became Operations Officer.

The results of this intensive training program were evident by the remarks made by Secretary of War Stimson on his visit to Tuskegee in February 1943, when he stated that the outfit was absolutely outstanding by any standards. Throughout the month of March, the pilots were not only further drilled in the fundamentals of aerial combat, formation flying, and night flying but, with the ground complement, were subjected to long forced marches and drilled in bivouac and air base maintenance procedures.

Finally on the morning of April 1, 1943, the 99th began making preparation for its departure from TAAF. The news of its leaving spread throughout the little town of Tuskegee, and the people who were there that day, both black and white, declared the squadron flyby was just a little more extraordinary than usual. The low altitude passover, the beautiful chandelle, and the tightness of formation was most special. The next days of April 2nd and 3rd, well wishers and friends gathered at the little depot at Cheehaw, and bid the men farewell, and good luck, as they boarded the troop train for Camp Shanks, New York . . . and to war . . .

The Early Days & The Birth of the 99th

ss Willa B. Brown and students at Harlem Airport, West Chicago. Her school known as the Coffey
nool, offered full range of CPTP and War Training Courses.

jor General W. R. Weaver, commanding the Southeast Air Corps Training Center, standing in the
dow of The Booker T. Washington monument, Tuskegee, Alabama, as he delivered the inaugural
ress, initiating the training of Negroes as military aviators for the United States Army Air Corps.

The late Judge William H. Hastie, Civilian Aide to the Secretary of War, whose continued opp tion to existing policies of discrimination, brought about many immediate changes in Air Co policy, including elimination of segregated bases, expansion of the Negro program to include formation of a fighter as well as a medium bomber group. He was termed by many to have b the father of the black air force.

Basic and advance flying school for Negro Air Corps Cadets, Tuskegee, Alabama. Major James A. Ellison returns the salute of Mac Ross, of Dayton, Ohio, as he passes the cadets lined up during review.

Tuskegee Army Air Field cadets line up with their BT-13s and AT-6s. January, 1942.

Tuskegee Army Field from 8,000 feet.

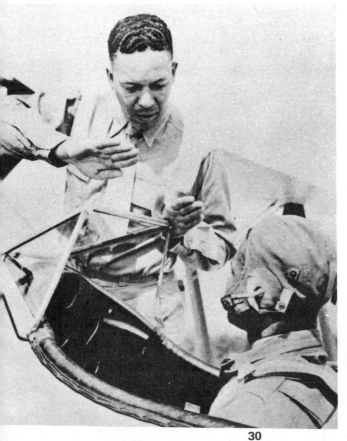

Charles A. "Chief" Andson in 1932 became t
first Negro to hold a co
mercial pilots license.
was selected as chief i
structor at Moton Fie
the primary phase of Cad
training at TAAF.

30

...nstructor Sherman T. Rose, explains to student Mack Hopkins how it should be done.

...vilian mechanics at Moton Field. All mechanics and primary instructors at this time were civil-
...s. Note PT-13s in background. PT-13s were later replaced by PT-17s, and 19s.

PRIMARY INSTRUCTORS, TUSKEGEE, DEC. 2, 1942. TOP: Bob Terry, John Young, Steven Charlie Fox, Roscoe Draper, Sherman Rose, James A. Hill, Adolph Moret, Ernest Henderson Mathew Plummer, Linkwood Williams, Lewis Jackson, "Chappie" James, Milton Crenshaw. BC TOM: Perry Young, Charlie Flowers, Claude Platt, "Chief" Anderson, C. R. Harris, Wend Lipscomb, J. E. Wright.

Charles W. Dryden
Moton Field in 1941. D
den was one of only th
cadets in the second cl
to graduate at Tuske
Army Air Field. Sho
here with PT-17 traine

32

CLASS 42C, The First. George S. Roberts, Capt. Benjamin O. Davis, Jr., Charles DeBow, Lt. Robert M. Long, (instructor) Mac Ross, and Lemuel R. Custis.

CLASS 42C, After Graduation. Top: Lt. Colonel Benjamin O. Davis Jr., 1st Lt. George S. Roberts, 1st Lt. Mac Ross, (bottom) 2nd Lt. Lemuel R. Custis, 2nd Lt. Charles DeBow.

CLASS 42D. Lieutenants: Charles W. Dryden, Sydney P. Brooks, and Clarence C. Jamison.

CLASS 42E. Top: Lieutenants: Lee Rayford, George L. Knox. (bottom) James B. Knighten, Sherman W. White.

34

CLASS 42F. This class went from CPTP to basic training. William A. Campbell, Willie Ashley, Langston Caldwell, Herbert Clark, George Bolling, Charles B. Hall, Graham Mitchell, Herbert Carter, Louis Purnell, Graham Smith, Allen G. Lane, Spann Watson, Faythe McGinnis, James T. Wiley, and Irwin Lawrence.

CLASS 42G Top: 2nd Lt. Richard "Bob" Davis, (on wings) Cassius "Baby" Harris, Willie Fuller, (standing: John W. "Jack" Rogers, Eugene "Cocky" King, John W. McClure, (bottom) Leon Roberts, Walter I. "Ghost" Lawson.

CLASS 42H. Top: John Morgan, Richard Ceasar, Edward Toppins, Robert Diez, Joseph Elsberry (bottom) Sam Bruce, Wilmore Leonard, James McCullin, Henry Perry.

CLASS 42I. Nathaniel Hill, Marshall Cabiness, Herman "Ace" Lawson, William T. Mattison, Joh Gibson, Elwood T. Driver, Price D. Rice, and Andrew "Jug" Turner.

LASS 42J. Jerome T. Edwards, Terry Charlton, Howard Baugh, Melvin "Red" Jackson.

LASS 42K. Top: Milton "Baby" Hall, Robert B. Tresville, Peter Verwayne, Wendell O. Pruitt, omeo Williams, (bottom) Edward C. Gleed, Richard Pullum, William "Wild Bill" Walker.

Basic Training. Cadets compare notes. October, 1942.

Cadets are assigned parachutes. Tuskegee Army Air Field, May 4, 1942.

tudent mechanics and instructor. Allison powered Curtis P-40s. Used during fighter transition raining by recent graduates.

North American AT-6 Texans above TAAF.

Ranking non-commissioned officers and enlisted mechanics install new dual radio set in BT-13 a
TAAF.

Crew Chief gives traine
final check. Tuskege
Army Air Field.

aptain Benjamin O. Davis,
r., climbing into AT-6.

ASS 43A. Clinton Mills, Quitman Walker, Andrew Maples, Chas. Stanton, George McCrumby,
mour McDaniel.

CLASS 43B. William H. "Wolf" Walker, Claude Govan, Walter Downs, James Polkinghorne, Joh Prowell, Roy Spencer, William Griffin.

CLASS 43C: Top: Elmer "Gloomy Gus" Gordon, Lloyd Singletary, Woodrow Crockett, Lawrence E. Dickson, W. M. Gordon, Alphonso Davis, Clarence Allen, Bowman, W. W. Sidat-Sing (bottom) Walter McCreary, Pearlee Saunders, Charles Jamerson, Alwayne Dumlap.

ASS 43D. Top: Ulysses Taylor, Harold Sawyer, Luke Weathers, Lewis Smith, Leonard Jack-
a, Curtis Robinson, Vernon Haywood, James Y. Carter, Walter Foreman, Charles Bailey,
arles I. Williams. (bottom) Heber Houston, James Brothers, Arnold Cisco, Paul Adams, Wil-
n Faulkner, Freddie Hutchins, Wilson Eagleson, Sidney Mosley.

SS 43E. TOP: Joseph P. Gomer, Felix, J. Kirkpatrick, Craig H. Williams, George E. Gray,
psey Morgan, Spurgeon Ellington, Albert Henning Jr., Dudley M. Watson, Milton R. Brooks,
y Sheppard, Charles H. Bussey, John F. Briggs. BOTTOM: Larry D. Wilkens, Maurice Esters,
er O. Miller, Luther H. Smith, Langdon Johnson, James A. Walker, John Suggs, and Cle-
ceau Givings.

CLASS 43F. TOP: J. J. Sloan, Walter Palmer, T. D. Moore, Not Known, Wylie Seldon, R
Alexander, Herb Harris, Milton Henry, and Alexander Bright. MIDDLE: F. D. Walker, Kirk
rick, Joe Lewis, W. H. Johnson, Wm. F. Williams, L. F. Turner, William Wilkerson. BOTT
Willie Hunter, Wayne Liggens, Hezekiah Lacy, Ted Wilson, Chas. McGhee, Oscar Kenny, Ric
Harris, and Weldon Groves.

CLASS 43G. Top: Lee A. Archer, Jr., William B. Ellis, Alva N. Temple, W.R. Bartley, Jam
Mason, Beryl Wyatt, Daniel "Chappie" James, Edward N. "Evil" Smith, Robert Nelson, Jo
Leahr, Harry Bailey, "Dopey" Hall, Robert H. Wiggins, Samuel L. Curtis, (bottom) Low
Steward, William R. Melton, Walter Drake Westmoreland, Maurice Page, Elmer W. Taylor
Holsclaw, Eddie A. McLaurin, Cornelius G. Rogers, Chubby Green, Claybourne A. Lockett,
Daniels.

44

CLASS 43H. Top: William McClenic, Alton Ballard, Roger Romine, Floyd Thompson, Alix. Pasquet, Norvell Stoudmire, Bernie Jefferson, Andrew Doswell, Charles Dunne, (middle) Charles Tate, Willard Woods, Starling Penn, Leon Purchase, Everett Bratcher, Samuel Jefferson, Harry Daniels, (bottom) Carrol Woods, George Taylor, Hubron Blackwell, William E. Hill, Smith W. Green, Hubert L. Jones.

CLASS 43I. The last full single engine class. TOP: W. N. Alsbrook, W. N. Morgan, A. Simmons, D. B. Ponder, C.L. Browder, N.V. Nelson, E. W. Watkins, and H. B. Scott. MIDDLE: C. B. Browne, E.L. Jones, N.W. Scales, C.W. Newman, M.A. Harris, C.F. May, P.G. Goodenough, and G.M. Rhodes.BOTTOM: R.H. Smith, W.D. Ross, C.N. Langston, C.E. Johnson, G.J. Haley, William Cross, C.B. Johnson.

CLASS 43J. The first combined single and multi-engine class.

CLASS 43K. Top: Funderburg, Hathcock, Harris, Dickson, Gamble, Lester, Williams, Bradfor, Friend, Pollard, Daniels, Hill, Lewis, Irving, Thompson, **(middle)** Wells, Highbaugh, Hille, Brazil, Hervey, Byrd, Cheatam, Kennedy, **(bottom)** black, Newsum, Fullbright, Lynn, White Harrison, Rogers, Bolden.

Charles DeBow, member of the first cadet class at TAAF, prior to flight in P-P-40F. Propeller man explains variable pitch prop.

Recent graduates at TAAF on the flight line. 2nd Lieutenants: Bill Melton, Maurice Page, Lowell C. Steward, Jack Holsclaw, and Buddy Lockett.

2nd Lieutenant Mac Ross became the first Negro member of the Catipillar Club, being forced to bail out of his P-40, during fighter transition training at TAAF. Mac was a member of the first cadet class.

Army Staff Nurses at TAAF receive basics in flight instruction as well. Shown here are: 1st Lt Della Rainey, 2nd Lt. Mencie Trotter, 2nd Lt. Abbie E. Voorhies, (Ross), and 2nd Lt. Ruth Speight.

48

Curtis P-40E Kittyhawks over TAAF. P-40s used during the later days in training sported a natural metal finish, with no national insignia.

Lt. Robert O'Neil admiring duplicate wings pinned on his mother Mrs. Sadie Brewington on Graduation Day at T.A.A.F.

A few 1944 classes at TAAF.

To Barbara — All the best — Jim Crowder

ISAB-13 MAR 44-1 CADET GRADUATION 44-C

A few more classes at TAAF.

Class 45C after completing primary phase of training at TAAF. Class was approximately one third this size upon completing advanced training.

AMERICA'S FIRST BLACK FIGHTER PILOTS — The original 99th Fighter Squadron, commanded by West Point graduate, Benjamin O. Davis, Jr., blazed the trail for other Black airmen trained at Tuskeegee, Ala., during World War II. Atlantan Charles Dryden, Lockheed-Georgia professional development administrator, is second from left on third row. The men are: front row, left to right, Herbert Carter, Lee Rayford, George Roberts, Col. B.O. Davis, Jr., commander, Lemuel Custis, Clarence Jamison, and Charles Hall; second row, Walter Lawson, Spann Watson, Allan Lane, Paul Mitchell, Leon Roberts, John Rogers, Louis Purnell, James Wiley, and Graham Smith; third row, Willie Ashley, Charles Dryden, Irwin Lawrence, William Campbell, Willie Fuller, Richard Davis, Sidney Brooks, Sherman White, and Richard C. Bolling. Dryden is a retired Air Force Lt. Col. Missing from photograph is James Knighten.

Top men in their graduating class were: 1st ranking 2nd Lt. Samuel Lynn, 2nd Lt. Frederick D. Funderburg, finishing second, and third ranking, 2nd Lt. Othel Dickson.

54

The 99th in Combat
& The 332nd Fighter Group

As the men of the 99th Fighter Squadron settled down for their rail journey to Camp Shanks, New York, many were still not convinced as to their destination. Upon arrival at the port of embarkation, followed by 10 days of intensive and tedious overseas preparation, it became certain that their departure from the country was but a matter of time. The order to board ship came April 15, 1943.

The selection of Lieutenant Colonel Benjamin O. Davis, Jr., as executive officer of the troop ship and its 4,000-man contingent was another Army first, for three quarters of his command were white. A black man serving in this capacity was unprecedented in U.S. Army history.

On the morning of April 24th, Africa was sighted and by late afternoon, the ship entered the harbor at Casablanca, Morocco. Colonel Davis prepared his troops, the total force of the 99th being nearly 400, for convoy through the city. In complete battle dress they arrived at the bivouac area where temporary quarters were established.

During the week, arrangements were made to move the unit to their assigned airfield, which they would share with the 27th Fighter Bomber Group. It took 20 hours to travel the 150 miles by rail; this, however, was normal, conditions being what they were. The ultimate destination was the little town of OuedN'ja (pronounced Wedenja) near Fez, between Casablanca and Tangier. Shortly after their arrival, the 99th was honored by a delegation headed by Lt. General Carl Spaatz, who was then commanding the North African Air Force; Brigadier General John K. "Uncle Joe" Cannon, commanding the North African Training Command; and Air Vice Marshal J.M. Robb of the Royal Air Force.

Pertaining to the squadron's stay at OuedN'ja, Colonel Davis remarked: "The duty here was probably the most pleasant we were to enjoy during our overseas tour. Cordial relations existed between the members of the 99th and the fighter bomber group nearby. Lieutenant Colonel John D. Stevenson, a friend of mine at the Academy, was commanding the unit. The pilots of the two groups engaged in impromptu dogfights to determine the relative superiority of the P-40 and the North American A-36. The enlisted men engaged in athletic competition, and the nearby town of Fez was found to be one of the most delightful that any of us had ever visited. For over a month, not one unpleasant incident arose between my men and those of the other groups frequenting the town."

The security felt by the men of the 99th also carried over to their equipment. Colonel Davis recalls, "Our planes and equipment were of the very best. We ferried in 27 new P-40 Warhawks from Casablanca, and for the first time, were able to experience the thrill of flying a brand new airplane." Previously all aircraft the men had flown, PT-13's to P-40's, were well used when received for training and fighter transition.

From all evidence, as verified by photos, and serial numbers, the Warhawks flown by the 99th during combat were L models, with a few F's later flown in as replacements. Photographs show absence of the carburetor scoop atop the cowl, characteristic of Allison-powered 40's, indicating the presence of Packard-built Merlin V-1650's of the F and L models. Former mechanics recall no Allison engines overseas, and serial numbers on aircraft assigned the 99th fell within the range of the L series, with the exception of the F's. No records list the use of any model later than L, though the N model was used in training.

Colonel Davis, in referring to the month of intensive training he and his squadron underwent to prepare them for the task ahead states: "Though Captain Roberts had nearly 600 hours, and I, 500, neither had any fighting experience. The Air Corps provided us with three veterans to hopefully compensate for this in the short time available. These men were a Major Keyes, previously stationed in England, Major Fachler, a veteran of the African campaign, and Colonel Phillip Cochran."

On May 31, 1943, the 99th arrived at Fordjouna in North Africa, and was to enter its final phase of training. It was attached to, but not a component of the 33rd Fighter Group, under the leadership of Colonel William "Spike" Momeyer. It was here that their most capable instructor was sent over by General Cannon. This man was Lieutenant Colonel Phil Cochran, "Mr. P-40," whose responsibility it was to indoctrinate the men to desert war, and dive bombing. Cochran had quickly gained a reputation as a tactical fighter genius in North Africa under General James Doolittle, and on January 10, had incurred the wrath of the entire Afrika Corps, by accurately placing a 500-pound bomb on the German headquarters in the Hotel Splendida in Kairouan. He was indeed as spectacular as he was capable.

Phil Cochran was probably better known to most Americans as "Colonel Flip Corkin" in Milton Caniff's popular wartime comic strip, "Terry & The Pirates." Cochran stated after the first few flights with the 99th, "These guys are a collection of natural-born dive bombers," and for a period of several weeks, every sortie consisted of six planes from Momeyer's group, and two P-40's of the 99th.

The first assignment of the 99th as wingmen to the 33rd came on June 2, 1943, a strafing mission against the heavily fortified island of Pantelleria. In reference to the squadron's entrance into combat, Colonel Davis said: "I personally believe that no unit in this war had gone into combat better trained or better equipped than the 99th. We were weak in the one respect aforementioned, and that was unfortunate in that we were unable to instill the confidence necessary for initial success in the men. On the other hand, this deficiency was balanced to a degree by the fact that my pilots averaged about 250 hours in a P-40, and a young pilot in those days who had 250 hours in a 40, before going into combat, was a hard man to find." The pilots assigned to this first mission were: Lieutenants Charles "C Buster" Hall, William "Wild Bill" Campbell, Clarence C. Jamison, and James T. "Little Flower" Wiley. In all, the mission was uneventful, and no enemy aircraft were sighted.

The 99th flew missions to Pantelleria for seven days without sighting the first enemy aircraft. They were now flying as an independent unit, no longer assigned as wingmen for the 33rd, but still operating with the group. Finally on the morning of June 9th, a flight led by Lieutenant Charles "A-Train" Dryden was attacked by a group of 12 Focke-Wulfs and Messerschmitts. Dryden's flight consisted of Lieutenants Lee "Suwannee" Rayford, Willie "Lord Beefley" Ashley, Spann Watson, Sidney Brooks, and Leon Roberts. The Jerries were escorting approximately 18 bombers coming in to attack the Allied invasion forces. Upon sighting the enemy, the P-40's climbed. The Germans peeled off from 12,000 feet, and dived through the Warhawks in loose formation of twos at better than 400 miles per hour. Two FW's caught Rayford's plane and riddled his right wing. Spann Watson came from Rayford's right, and fired a burst at the two Germans. The Nazis flipped over and broke away. Willie Ashley had lost considerable altitude, having gone into a spin, and upon recovering found an FW crossing his sights. He got in a raking burst, and the German went into a flat smoking glide down toward the sea. The other enemy planes turned and ran for Sicily. Ashley pursued the 190 until enemy ground fire forced him back, and as a result probably lost the opportunity to become the first Negro pilot to score a victory.

The air assault on Pantelleria had begun on May 30, 1943. By June 11, the island surrendered, and for the first time in history, air power alone had completely destroyed all enemy resistance. No less than 16 sorties a day were carried out by Negro flyers during their nine days of activity against the island. Lieutenant William Campbell, during this assault, won the distinction of being the first colored man ever to drop a bomb on an enemy of the United States. Upon returning to base, Campbell declared, "I was scared but determined to stay on the wing of the leader even if he carried me into the front door of enemy headquarters!" His return from the mission was without serious incident though he taxied his plane into a bomb crater, which had been left by American bombers during an attack on the field before it fell into Allied hands. Campbell's squadron mates consoled him, realizing it could have happened to the most seasoned veteran. This was little consolation to Campbell, however, who had more hours in P-40's than other unit members, and had never scratched a military aircraft.

Allied forces now turned their strength toward Sicily, the doorstep to Italy. The 99th moved to El Haouria, on the Cape Bon Peninsula, and began operating as a component of the 324th Fighter Group, under the command of Colonel Leonard C. Lydon, which was already involved in the Sicilian campaign. The role of the 99th was to escort medium bombers to the western sector of Sicily. Their first mission in this new role was July 1, 1943.

It was on July 2 that the 99th entered the victory column. Six P-40's were assigned the role of escorting 16 B-25's whose mission was to bomb the Castelvetrano Airfield. The following account was given by Lieutenant Charles B. Hall, of Brazil, Indiana: "It was my eighth mission, but the first time I had seen the enemy close enough to shoot at. I saw two FW-190's following the Mitchells just after the bombs were dropped. I headed for the space between the fighters and bombers and managed to turn inside the jerries. I fired a long burst and saw my tracers penetrate the second aircraft. He was turning to the left, but suddenly fell off and headed straight into the ground. I followed him down and saw him crash. He raised a big cloud of dust." General Dwight Eisenhower, who arrived shortly thereafter personally congratulated him, and also praised the performance of the squadron to date. Thus Lieutenant Hall gained the distinction of becoming the first Negro member of the Army Air Corps to paint a swastika on his ship. "Buster" Hall had attended Illinois State Teachers College, and enlisted in the Air Corps in November, 1941. Then Captain George Roberts, upon recalling Hall as a pilot, states: "Buster had one problem if it could be considered as such. He was totally without fear. With the outstanding qualities he possessed as a pilot, he would probably have become an ace, though our contact with the enemy was minimal and our aircraft of inferior capabilities. Buster would have found a way." As it was, Hall's victory total ceased at three. He was returned to the States before the 99th acquired P-51's. His commander's assumptions likely would have been correct had Hall's tour continued.

Also on July 2nd, Lieutenant Walter I. "Ghost" Lawson scored a probable. Lawson acquired his rather unusual nickname under rather tragic circumstances. Only a short time before graduation, on June 8, 1942, he and cadet Robert "Red" Dawson were sharpening their skills in an AT-6. Dawson, in the forward cockpit, decided to fly under a bridge. Unknown to him, high tension lines stretched beneath the structure, and the AT was cut in half upon impact. Dawson was killed, and Lawson, also presumed dead, was found wandering in a state of shock about a mile from the crash scene.

The success of Lieutenant Hall was accompanied by sadness. The 99th suffered its first combat casualties when Lieutenants Sherman White and James McCullin were hit by enemy ground fire on missions earlier that day, and reported missing in action. Their deaths were later confirmed.

On July 10, 1943, the invasion of Sicily commenced, and throughout that day, the 99th made numerous divebombing missions and strafing attacks, as well as escorting medium bombers of the Twelfth Tactical Air Force. That afternoon Lieutenant George "Cool Papa" Bolling, whose aircraft was severely damaged by flak, was forced to ditch in the Mediterranean, and after floating for 24 hours in his dinghy, was picked up by a destroyer. Several days later he boarded a ship for North Africa, and was returned to his squadron. On this same date, the 99th completed its operation with the 324th Fighter Group. During its attachment, which lasted for 11 days, it flew 175 sorties, had one confirmed victory, and two probables. The squadron was attached as air support to General Montgomery's Eighth Army for the next eight days, and on July 19, again joined the 33rd Fighter Group, moving to Licata, Sicily, located on the Mediterranean Sea.

July brought the first group of replacements for the 99th. Arriving on the 23rd were: Lieutenants Howard Baugh, Edward Toppins, John Morgan, and John Gibson. Arriving shortly thereafter were Lieutenants Herman "Ace" Lawson, and Clinton "Beau" Mills. These last two were scheduled to arrive via Military Air Transport, but due to unexplained military confusion, they were stranded in Brazil for three weeks. They finally caught up with the 99th on July 22nd, after having departed Oscoda, Michigan, on June 28. In Michigan they had trained with the newly formed 332nd Fighter Group. "Ace" recalls the fiasco: "I don't know yet how we ended up in Brazil, but the Air Corps brass there not only never heard of the 99th, nor were they interested in finding it. When we finally reported to Colonel Davis, nearly a month late, he still hadn't gotten our orders, and was quite surprised, though pleased to see us."

On August 11, 1943, tragedy again struck the 99th. The squadron was just starting a mission and the planes were slipping into formation. War correspondent Edgar T. Rouzeau reported Lieutenant Samuel Bruce's comments: "I was just getting positioned at 1,500 feet when another plane far to my right apparently developed engine trouble, lost height, and veered left into my path. A collision seemed unavoidable, but I nosed upward for a split second and thought we missed. My propeller chopped the tail off the other plane flown by Lieutenant Graham H. Mitchell, who didn't have a chance to save himself. My plane kept flying at the same level and I was able to bail out. I was amazed the chute opened in time. Jumping seconds later, I wouldn't have made it. Although dazed, I saw Mitchell's plane burning nearby, he had been killed."

In late August of 1943, squadron commander Benjamin O. Davis, Jr., was relieved of his command to return to the United States to assume command of the newly formed 332nd Fighter Group, now training at Selfridge Field. "Spanky, the destiny of the squadron is in your hands." With those parting words, Colonel Davis left the 99th in the charge of Captain George Roberts. The position was not new to Roberts, who had been the original commander of the unit. As the C-54 departed from the airfield in southern Sicily, Captain Roberts immediately set forth his plans for squadron operation. "The 99th will never have as fine a commander as the skipper. I hated to see him go." Roberts cemented relations between officers, and enlisted men. He issued orders they bring their grievances directly to him, and with uncanny insight into the capacities of his men, was able to utilize this ability in handing out assignments with utmost efficiency.

To date, the 99th, the Army's stepchild, had been shoved around, bypassed, and virtually ignored. Adverse publicity began to filter through both military and civilian sources. Throughout the Sicilian and Salerno campaign, the 99th flew missions without sighting enemy aircraft. There were pilots in the squadron who had finished their allotted missions and gone back to America without ever firing a shot at an enemy plane. Lack of aerial victories led to the questioning of the aggressiveness of the unit. The late Ernie Pyle, in his book *Brave Men*, wrote: "Their job was to dive bomb, and not get caught in a fight. The 99th was very successful at this, and that's the way it should be." Pyle goes on to say, "For several reasons our dive bombers didn't have much trouble with German fighters. First of all, the Luftwaffe was weak over there at the time. Then too, the dive bombers' job was to work on the infantry front lines, so they seldom got back to where the German fighters were."

Captain Roberts, in relating a visit by General H.H. Arnold to the base, shortly after his resumption of command, said: "I never felt so bad in all my life. It was extremely difficult for me as he stood there discrediting, and maligning the men who were doing their best under the circumstances. Whether right or wrong in his assessment of the unit, his manner was not what should be expected from the Chief of the Air Corps."

On the occasion of Colonel Davis' return to the States, *Time* magazine on September 20, 1943 published an article entitled, "Experiment Proved?". It contained not only an account of an interview with Davis, but also hints and rumors about the current status of the squadron. So little operational data on the 99th had reached Washington, the magazine observed, that it was impossible to form a conclusive estimate of its abilities. "It has apparently seen little action, compared to many other units," the magazine reported, and "unofficial reports from the Mediterranean Theater have suggested that the top air command was not altogether satisfied with the squadron's performance. There is said to be a plan to attach it to the Coastal Air Command, in which it would be assigned to routine convoy cover."

On September 30, 1943, the *New York Daily News,* in a feature article by John O'Donnell further clouded the picture claiming that: "Although thousands of Negro soldiers have been drafted, only one outfit, the 99th Air Squadron, has been engaged in actual combat. This had brief action in Africa but has since broken up and its members returned to the United States for training purposes."

Protests and queries on the *Time* story, and the completely erroneous statements of the *Daily News,* began to come into the War Department at about the same time the official theater reports arrived. The Group Commander of the 33rd Fighter Group, under which the 99th entered combat, had this to say regarding their performance, compared to other squadrons in his group: "The ground discipline in accomplishing and executing orders is excellent. Air discipline has not been completely satisfactory. The ability to work and fight as a team has not yet been acquired. Their formation flying has been excellent until attacked by the enemy, when the squadron seems to disintegrate. On numerous instances when assigned to dive bomb a specified target, though anti-aircraft fire was light or inaccurate, they chose a secondary target which was undefended. On one specified occasion, the 99th turned back before reaching the target because of the weather. The other squadron went on to the target and pressed home the attack." Colonel Momeyer continues, "Based on the performance of the 99th Fighter Squadron to date, it is my opinion that they are not of the fighting caliber of any squadron in this Group." General House, Commander of the Twelfth Air Support Command, stated that "In the opinion of officers in all professions, including medical, the Negro type has not the proper reflexes to make a first-class fighter pilot." He recommended that the 99th be assigned to the Northwest African Coastal Air Force, and equipped with P-39's so that its P-40's could be used as replacements for the "active groups," and if and when a Negro group was completely formed it could be kept in the States for defense command duties, thereby releasing a white fighter group for overseas movement.

General House's report was forwarded to General Henry Arnold, whose pessimism concerning the Negro program had been common knowledge from the beginning. The general consensus of opinion by Air Corps brass was that the 99th, as well as the three fighter squadrons in training be relegated to a rear defense area, and that the continuation of plans for a Negro bombardment group be abandoned. The War Department, however, recommended this be done only with President Roosevelt's approval.

The Air Corps attached to its recommendation, an analysis indicating that the 99th had required eight months of training in comparison with three months for white units, and that its requirements in supervisory personnel had been "completely out of proportion to the results achieved." They failed to include in their analysis, however, that the illogical, unorthodox arrangements through which the 99th completed its training, with all the attendant delays and problems of supervision, now charged against the squadron, were in fact resultant from the Air Corps' own negative, and biased procedures in forming the unit.

In view of all the controversy being stirred, it was decided by General George C. Marshall, that G-3, and a Senate Advisory Committee be directed to analyze the entire Negro program, ground as well as air.

On October 16, 1943, Colonel Davis, who had returned to the United States to take over command of the 332nd, was brought to Washington before the Senate Advisory Committee, to answer the charges against the performance of the 99th. The Colonel began his answers to the committee's queries by saying that the main part of General House's letter was quoted from Colonel Momeyer's report, which was based upon an opinion. Davis went on to say that the squadron had entered combat with certain handicaps. Because no one had combat experience, there were certain mistakes arising out of inexperience, during the squadron's first missions. For these he would offer no excuse. On the squadron's first encounter with the enemy over Pantelleria, it failed to maintain a flight of sixes, breaking down to twos. There was one occasion when the squadron failed to dive bomb a target. Colonel Davis had led that mission and turned back on account of weather. This was substantiated, and no secondary target was involved. That the squadron had a reputation for disintegrating when jumped, came as a surprise to him, for only the one incident, the one which he had mentioned, had been called to his attention. If there was a lack of aggressiveness initially, it was only at first. The question as to the stamina of his men was brought up, and Davis stated that on August 15, he had requested that his men have 48 hours off due to general fatigue, but he thought the circumstances should be considered. The squadron had operated continuously for two months without receiving replacement pilots, although the standard set up for that time, was four a month. Consequently the 99th had only 26 pilots as compared to 30 to 35 in other squadrons in the area. On heavy days therefore, his pilots flew from three to six missions. If he had a full quota of men, perhaps the strain would have been lessened. The impression that the squadron was not aggressive had been brought to his attention again. "I carried out my mission. If given a mission to bomb a target, I went ahead and bombed it."

Upon analysis of all facts presented, and Colonel Davis' testimony, the War Department, and G-3, recommended that the Army send the 332nd Fighter Group to the Mediterranean area in order to provide a "just and reasonable test" of the value of large Negro air units in combat, and that plans for the formation of a Negro medium bombardment group be expedited and carried out as planned. . . .

During the height of the controversy stateside, the most significant event in the first year of the 99th, and indeed one of the most important in the history of the Negro air program, was the quiet but effective assimilation of the 99th into the 79th Fighter Group, and the integration of the fighting skills of the two races in an Army combat unit. On October 7th, the 99th joined them at Foggia, Italy, and moved with the 79th to Madna on November 19th. The group was now flying 36 to 48 sorties a day, and all the arguments about the two races being unable to function together proved groundless. The men flew, worked, and fought together, and the group's official newspaper, *The Falcon*, in its press releases, made it impossible to realize the 99th was other than just another squadron in the group. Much of the success of the integration should be accredited to Colonel Earl E. Bates, the CO of the 79th. To a man, the 99th felt Colonel Bates was a fair, impartial thinker, with only his men at heart, and the success of the group. Colonel Bates mixed the squadrons on missions, and each of the four squadrons assumed identical duties. On November 30, the 79th flew 26 missions, a new record. Of these, the 99th flew nine.   Pilots of the 99th under now Major George S. Roberts gained in experience and confidence in their association with the 79th. After two months, the 99th, which in the absence of a means of direct comparison, had thought of itself as a combat-wise veteran of the Pantellerian and Sicilian campaigns, now found that it had learned a great deal more through the adoption of the flight tactics, takeoff system, and formations of the older, more experienced group. "With these changes comes more experience and with the experience comes confidence. These two attributes are precisely what pilots of the 99th Squadron are getting."

Shortly after joining the 79th, an incident occurred which further cemented the relations between the 99th and its new mates.

Lieutenant Alva N. Temple, perhaps the quietest member of the 99th, gained the admiration and respect of the Desert Falcon Group, when on takeoff, his landing gear was damaged by a collision. With one gear partially retracted and being fully aware of his plight, he continued the mission, and returned his damaged Warhawk to the field, pancaking in with but the loss of his port wing.

The unity, and spirit in the squadron, was hard to describe, and as written by War Correspondent Walter White, in his book, *A Wind Is Rising*, "This was democracy in action, and seemed more nearly achieved in these moments than it had ever been before, though it is tragic that a war of such proportions and destructiveness had apparently been necessary to cause Americans in isolated instances like this one to forego race prejudice. . . ."

Pilots of the 99th, eligible to return to the United States after flying 50 missions, began to request longer tours, and the men felt that they had finally joined the air team. However, to date the 99th still had only one confirmed victory after completion of six months' duty. This was soon to change.

On January 22, 1944, Allied forces landed at Anzio, the battle for Sicily ended, the battle of Italy just begun, and the Twelfth Air Force was made responsible for isolating the battle area to prevent enemy forces from bringing up reinforcements and supplies necessary for a successful counterattack. The 79th FG was assigned to support the ground troops by dive bombing and strafing rail yards, troop concentration, highways, bridges, ports, and supply centers. The opportunity came for the 99th on the morning of January 27th. A flight led by Captain Clarence Jamison spotted a group of enemy fighters over the Anzio beachhead. The flight broke formation, and though outnumbered nearly two to one, in less than four minutes, had downed five enemy aircraft. That afternoon three more enemy aircraft were destroyed by the 99th. The flight, led by Lieutenant James T. Wiley, thus brought the day's total to eight. Lieutenant Samuel "Lizzard" Bruce of Seattle, Washington, was killed during the action, and though last seen chasing two Focke-Wulfs, it was generally agreed that an RAF Spitfire mistakingly shot him down. On this day, the 79th FG, flying top cover for the 99th scored one victory, five Jerries by the "Red Guerrillas" of the 33rd FG, and nine by RAF Spitfires.

On January 28, the 99th was credited with four more, Captain Charles "Buster" Hall confirming two. Between February 5th and 10th, the 99th bagged another four, bringing their total to date: 17 confirmed, four probables, and six damaged. They had lost a total of eight men, three to enemy action. Captain Hall was credited with three victories, Lieutenants Diez, Eagleson, and Custis, each with two, Lieutenants Driver, Mills, Ashley, Jackson, Toppins, Bailey, Leon Roberts each with one, with Lieutenants Baugh and Allen sharing another. The 99th had flown 390 missions, 2,528 sorties, and several men had flown more than 80 missions.

The success of the 99th now brought official commendation from sources previously so negative on its future. A message from General Arnold read in part: "The results of the 99th Fighter Squadron during the past two weeks, particularly since the Anzio landing, are very commendable. My best wishes for their continued success." General John K. Cannon of the Twelfth Air Force, landed his A-36 at the base to personally congratulate the unit, and extend his pleasure over their success to Major Roberts. In responding to the General's well wishes, Roberts said: "We're not the best, but we're as good as any the U.S. Army puts out. That's what's important."

On April 1, 1944, the squadron was reorganized, and Captain Erwin B. Lawrence, of Cleveland, Ohio, succeeded Major Roberts as commander. Roberts returned to the States after completing 78 missions. During his tour with the 99th, Roberts had engaged in four dogfights, and though he made no claims of his own, members of his squadron can account for two Jerries which should have been his. Spanky jokingly said, "As long as they're disposed of, I won't worry about who downed them."

The squadron next moved to Cercola, Italy, and was released from operations with the 79th. The men were sorely disappointed, as they had attributed so much of their success to the group. They were now attached to the 324th Fighter Group once again, and were assigned to bomber escort duty, the Italian campaign virtually over. General Ira C. Eaker, Mediterranean Allied Commander, upon inspection of the squadron on April 20th, said, "By the magnificent showing your fliers have made since coming to this theater, and especially in the Anzio beachhead operation, you have not only won the plaudits of the Air Force, but have earned the opportunity to apply your talent to much more advanced work than was at one time planned for you."

Following the 99th's short attachment to the 324th, they were for a brief period assigned to the 86th Fighter Group. Neither of these assignments were as rewarding as was their duty with the 79th, and more nearly paralleled their stay with the 33rd. They were again operating as an individual squadron, and were never a part of group operations. On June 29th, they left for Orbetello, Italy, to join the all-Negro 332nd Fighter Group, and at Rametelli, Italy, on July 2, were immediately integrated into the four squadron organization, which had just acquired P-51C Mustangs.

The 332nd Fighter Group

At the same time the 99th Fighter Squadron was departing Tuskegee for overseas assignment, the remaining pilot force, along with the 96th Service Group, was preparing for transfer to Selfridge Field, Michigan, for combat training. Oscoda, a sub-base some 200 miles north was to be utilized as a bomb and gunnery range, thus making the combined facilities the largest Army Air Corps base for the training of Negroes.

The 332nd Fighter Group, activated at TAAF on October 13, 1942 with only eight officers and 12 enlisted men, accomplished little in the way of training. The lack of trained Negro personnel, the extreme shortage of airplanes and parts, as well as the lack of supervisors and instructors again contributing to the delays. The cadre for the 332nd had been the 100th Fighter Squadron, activated on May 15, 1942 under the leadership of Lieutenant Mac Ross. Upon departing Tuskegee on March 27, 1943 for Mt. Clemons, Michigan, personnel were rapidly transferred to the group, and by the end of April, the 332nd had received its full complement of men, resulting in the formation of the 301st and 302nd Fighter Squadrons, under the leadership of Lieutenants Charles DeBow, and William T. Mattison respectively. Following Ross, who had been appointed as group operations officer, was Lieutenant George Knox as CO of the 100th.

On October 19, 1942, Lieutenant Colonel Sam Westbrook of Albany, Georgia, was selected to command the 332nd. Many felt that a white Southerner would lack the dedication necessary to fulfill his duty. It was a new experience for the Colonel as well as the men, and though he did little to endear himself to them, he performed his duties in creditable fashion. ·

Though a northern location had hopefully eliminated some of the discriminatory policies which could arise, racial conflicts did occur at the base, and failure to provide to the Negroes, services available to white personnel, was a major source of discontent.

In June, 1943, Colonel Robert R. "Get to your guns" Selway took over command of the group, and within a comparatively short time, the 332nd developed into a functioning combat unit. All of the pilots had undergone their required 20 hours of transitional fighter training in P-40's while at Tuskegee, but further delays at Selfridge plagued the program. The original order to equip them with P-40's was cancelled midway through their combat training, and after considering the use of P-47's, the decision to switch to P-39's was made by the Air Corps. This resulted in retraining pilots and crews.

By early September, the transition to Airacobras was complete, and most of the pilots desired the feel of the lighter, more nimble aircraft. Initially, P-40C's of the First Air Force were utilized. In most cases, these were ready for "retirement," and a few were painted with the characteristic shark mouth, giving rise to reports by the Negro press that "Black airmen are flying the remains of the Flying Tigers!" Master Sergeant James Jones, former Line Chief of the 100th FS, recalls the condition of the Selfridge Field Tomahawks originally flown by the men: "In a few cases, we had to hold hoses on those old Allisons due to overheating while warming up. It was a shame to think that our boys were expected to fly those things. It was all my men could do to keep them airworthy. We lived in continual fear that someone wouldn't return due to a failure beyond our control. When they returned from a flight, it appeared quite frequently as though they'd flown through an oil storm." During the first week in Michigan, two men were lost. Lieutenant Wilmeth Sidat-Singh was forced to bail out over Lake Huron after his aircraft burst into flames, and Lieutenant Jerome T. Edwards was killed at Oscoda under similar conditions. Both were flying P-40C's. Fortunately as the group received its full complement of men, the obsolete C's were phased out in favor of the F's, and finally the P-39's.

On October 7, 1943, Lieutenant Colonel Benjamin O. Davis, Jr., replaced Colonel Selway as commander. The group was to profit from the overseas experiences of Davis and several combat veterans of the 99th, who were also transferred to the group.

Departing Camp Patrick Henry, Virginia, on January 3, 1944, via troop transports, the 332nd FG arrived at Taranto, Italy, between January 29 and February 3, with its three full squadrons. On February 5, the 100th FS became operational and participated in its first mission. The group was assigned to harbor and coastal patrol as well as convoy escort missions with the Twelfth Air Force. These duties were previously assigned to the 81st Fighter Group, which now had moved to the Fourteenth Air Force in the China, Burma, India Theater. By the 15th of February, all three squadrons had entered combat, and were equipped with P-39Q Airacobras.

On February 15th, Lieutenants Larry Wilkins and Weldon Groves of the 302nd made the group's initial contact with the enemy. Though getting off several bursts at a JU-88 off Geata Point, they failed to score any hits. On February 17th, Lieutenants Roy Spencer and William R. Melton, also of the 302nd, scored hits, knocking out the port engine of a JU-88 near Ponsa Point, but as told by Lieutenant Melton, "Those Airacobras just didn't have enough to close in, and at that altitude, he just walked away from us."

The experience gained in early operations soon enabled the group to widen its activities, and Washington being made aware of this, had planned and preferred to re-equip the 332nd with P-63 Kingcobras, the new and improved version of the P-39, but delays in proving and delivering this plane, plus General Eaker's urging, provided the group with P-47's. Even before the fall of Rome, Allied Commanders decided that strategic bombing of supply centers, bridges, and harbor installations was the most effective means of crippling the German war effort, and many tactical fighter groups were relieved and assigned to strategic bomber escort duty. General Eaker informed Washington that on the basis of the group's performance, he was "very anxious" for the 332nd to be re-equipped with Thunderbolts at the same time the older groups in the theater were changed over. Further time was lost, however, over the P-63 question. By the time the group had received its orders to transfer to the Fifteenth Air Force, the 325th FG, which had been using P-47's since May, was being re-equipped with P-51's. The 332nd inherited their "Razorback P-47D's, and hastily overpainted the black and yellow checkerboard design with their newly designated all red tail surfaces. They became part of the 306th Fighter Wing, and flew their first mission on June 7, 1944.

The first big day for the "Red Tails" came on June 9, 1944, when the group was credited with five victories. As described by Lieutenant Wendell O. Pruitt, of the 302nd, who was credited with the first kill: "We were assigned to fly top cover for heavy bombers. On approaching the Udine area, a flock of Me-109's were observed making attacks from 5 o'clock on a formation of B-24's. Each enemy aircraft made a pass at the bombers and fell into a left rolling turn. I rolled over, shoved everything forward and closed in on a 109 at about 475 mph. I waited as he shallowed out of a turn, gave him a couple of two second bursts, and watched him explode." Aside from Pruitt's victory, Lieutenant Fredrick Funderburg was credited with two, Lieutenant Melvin "White" Jackson, one, and Lieutenants Charles Bussey and William "Chubby" Green shared one.

Upon recalling the events of the day, former Staff Sergeant Samuel Jacobs, Lieutenant Pruitt's Crew Chief, relates the following: "We had been flying Thunderbolts for about a week. Some representatives from Republic Aviation, and some Air Corps brass had been scheduled to arrive and teach us how to fly, and crew the 47's. However, by the time they had arrived, our Engineering Officers and Line Chiefs had schooled us on everything we needed to know, and we'd already flown a couple of missions. I remember this Major standing atop a munitions carrier telling us "boys" all about the "flying bathtub" and how it should never be slow rolled below a thousand feet, due to its excessive weight. No sooner had he finished his statement than "A" flight was returning from its victorious mission. Down on the deck, props cutting grass, came Lieutenants Pruitt and his wingman Lee Archer, nearly touching wings. Lieutenant Pruitt pulled up into the prettiest victory roll you'd ever see, with Archer right in his pocket, as the Major screamed, "YOU CAN'T DO THAT!!!!"

On June 24th, Captain Robert B. Tresville, a recent West Point graduate, who had assumed leadership of the 100th FS, devised a strafing mission, the purpose of which was to disrupt the German supply lines at Aircasea-Pinerola in northern Italy. He felt that coming in low over the Tyrrhenian Sea would not only escape radar detection, but also catch the Jerries napping. As related by his wingman, Lieutenant Willard L. Woods: "Bob was an excellent pilot, and held the respect of all the men. The success of this strike was based upon ideal weather conditions, and surprise. The mission was in most minds considered rather risky. It called for an extremely long flight over water at zero altitude, and returning home down the coast. Had the weather held, the mission might have succeeded. This was not to be, and upon approaching Corsica, the ceiling fell in on us. I was flying Bob's right wing, with Dempsey Morgan, and Spurgeon Ellington on his left. Bob kept motioning for me to get it up a little, but I didn't realize until told later that my wing tanks were kicking up water. Shortly after sighting the coast, Bob, evidently disoriented, was looking at his map. The next thing I realized my plane pitched slightly upward, as Bob hit the water. We not only lost an exceptional man, but never were able to find the target."

The last major achievement before releasing their P-47's came on June 25, 1944, when the group, being led by Captain Joseph Elsberry, came upon a German destroyer in Trieste Harbor. The ship threw up a massive barrage, as a flight consisting of Elsberry, Lieutenants Joe Lewis, Charles Dunne, Gwynne Pierson and Wendell Pruitt, went in. Pruitt made a hit, setting the ship afire. Pierson made another direct hit, evidently to the magazine, as the ship exploded. Fifteenth Air Force was quite skeptical, as the planes carried no bombs on this mission, but wing cameras on the Thunderbolts provided the stark evidence of the accuracy of their machine gun fire. The P-47's accomplished what no other fighter group could claim, which made the feat even more satisfying.

The 332nd was not in its P-47's long enough to really feel at home in them. During the last week in June a few natural metal P-47D-25's (bubble canopy) were ferried in from North Africa as replacements. In the case of the original Thunderbolts used by the group, all were olive and gray razorbacks, with the buzz numbers of the 325th Fighter Group still intact. Almost simultaneously, however, the 332nd began receiving P-51B's and C's from the 31st and 325th which were now switching to P-51D's. The 51's were all natural metal, the distinguishing differences between the squadrons, which all carried the complete red tail surfaces, being the nose bands and trim tabs.

During this transition to Mustangs, the 99th joined the Group at their new base at Ramitelli, Italy, on July 3. The transfer brought new problems. Pilots of the 99th felt that the War Department was reverting to segregation policies practiced in the States. They felt that transferring them to the 332nd was based purely on race, particularly since they believed they were to become part of the 79th Fighter Group, and actually had received a few P-47's before being released from the group. Many felt that a larger segregated Negro group would mean loss of identity. Many veterans of 50 or more missions were fearful of becoming wingmen to men with no combat experience at all. On the other hand, the 332nd feared the experienced pilots of the 99th would be assigned all the responsible positions. Soon, however, all fears proved groundless, and the union was accomplished. The 99th was allowed to keep its dinstinctive "A" designation on each of its aircraft, with the identification number divided by the national insignia, a carryover from the Twelfth Air Force. They were assigned dark blue and white checkerboard nose bands just aft of the red spinners.

The new home for the 332nd Fighter Group at Ramitelli was quite adequate. Being the only active four squadron combat group in the Air Corps was also unique to the 332nd. An enormous building, once owned by an Italian landowner, provided spacious quarters for their operations headquarters. The only landing strip was constructed of steel mat, running from east to west. The 99th and 100th Squadrons were at opposite sides of the east end, with the 301st and 302nd at opposing sides of the other end. The direction of takeoff was usually toward the Adriatic Sea, being only a precariously short distance from the end of the mat. The men therefore became quite proficient at taking off with the minimum amount of usable space.

On July 11, 1944, Captain Mac Ross, former Group Operations Officer, was killed during transition training in one of the newly acquired Mustangs. On the same day, the youngest member of the original 99th, Captain Leon Roberts of Pritchard, Alabama, was killed. Having completed 116 missions without receiving a scratch, his P-51 peeled out of formation at 30,000 feet and crashed, giving speculation to the probability that the altitude got him.

On July 12, Captain Joseph Elsberry of Langston, Oklahoma, scored a triple. To date, only one Negro pilot had totaled three victories, but Elsberry became the first to accomplish this in one mission. B-17's of the 5th Bombardment Wing, just after crossing the coast of France, were attacked by perhaps 30 FW-190's. The heavies being about three minutes late for their rendezvous with the Red Tail escorts, necessitated a slow 360-degree turn by the fighters to await the Fortresses. In the meantime, the Jerries took advantage of the lag to strike. On spotting the enemy aircraft, Elsberry, of the 301st FS, ordered his Mustangs to drop tanks. When the 190's saw the 51's, they turned from the bombers, leaving themselves exposed from the rear. Diving at greater speed, the P-51's overtook the enemy and as related by Elsberry: "I picked out a Focke-Wulf within good shooting range and fired away. A mild explosion occurred midship. He rolled over and headed straight down. A second 190 crossed at about a 70-degree angle and I turned inside him. He began to smoke and fell into a dive toward the ground. I followed the third through a series of split 'S' maneuvers as he tried to avoid me. We started at 11,000 feet, ending at about 2,000 before I broke off my attack. He must have either been hit, or thought I was still behind him. Just before reaching the ground, he tried to pull up, but ran out of sky." Eight days later, Elsberry scored his fourth victory, another FW-190 while escorting B-24's of the 47th Bombardment Wing in the Munich area. While in hot pursuit of still another, and determined to make a kill, he was forced to pull up to avoid running into a mountain peak. "This was the last time I engaged an enemy aircraft at close range and my failure to register this victory meant the difference of being cited as an ace."

On July 15, the Group flew its first four squadron escort mission and on July 17, while escorting the 304th Bomb Wing to the Avignon marshaling yards, scored three victories on enemy planes attempting to intercept the bombers. The following day, 11 more victories were confirmed, with Lieutenant Clarence D. "Lucky" Lester, of the 100th FS, scoring the second triple for the Group. Captain Andrew D. "Jug" Turner, the new CO of the squadron, had just made a pass at a Me-109, and was climbing for altitude when he saw Lester in the midst of a group of 109's. By the time "Miss-Pelt," Lester's Mustang, had broken from the scramble, three Messerschmitts were in flames.

Lieutenant Jack Holsclaw of Portland, Oregon, gained two of the victories of the day, and Lieutenant Lee A. "Buddy" Archer scored his first. Archer, wingman to the flamboyant Wendell Pruitt, was to run his total to five, and become the only member of the 332nd to achieve "Ace" status. However, some controversy arose over one of his claims, and though listed on some official records with five victories, most do not include him. His second victory was two days later, on July 20, with the last three, including the controversial one, on October 12, 1944. On this particular mission, nine enemy aircraft were destroyed in the air, 26 on the ground. Wendell Pruitt was credited with two, Captain Milton "Mother" Brooks with one, as were Lieutenants William "Chubby" Green, Luther Smith, and Roger Romine. The Group was escorting B-24's of the 47th Bombardment Wing. The 302nd was the low squadron and flew to the extreme right of the others. Archer describes the action from this point: "We had just crossed Lake Balaton, when I spied a group of enemy aircraft at two o'clock and climbing. I called in the bandits and Pruitt was the first to pick up my message. He peeled off, rolled over, and dived for the enemy aircraft. There were a couple of He-111's and about 12 Me-109's. Two Messerschmitts were flying abreast. I tore the wing off one with a long burst. The other slid in behind Pruitt, I pulled up, zeroed in, hit the gun button, and watched him explode." It was the third that caused the controversy. Pruitt was chasing a 109, and his guns jammed. Archer followed the Jerry down, and as he explains: "I don't know whether he was damaged by Pruitt or not, but he appeared to be trying to land. I opened up at ground level, hit him with a long volley, and he crashed. Flak and small arms fire forced me out of there in a hurry."

71

During the winter of '44, the 332nd, newest member of the Fifteenth Fighter Command, was employed largely as escort for heavies attacking oil installation, marshaling yards, and ordnance plants in Germany, Austria, and Czechoslovakia. Several long-range escort missions were conducted to the Ploesti and Bucharest oil refineries in Rumania. Strafing attacks against enemy airdromes, troop concentrations, railroads, highways, and river traffic in central Europe and the Balkans were also carried out during this period.

Initially, the 332nd had not been called upon by the Air Corps commanders, because of lack of confidence in them, but now morale rose among the ground crews and pilots as more important missions were being assigned. Major General Nathan Twining, and Brigadier General Dean C. Strother of Fifteenth Air Force Headquarters, visited and praised the efficiency, and as more enemy aircraft were downed, everyone enjoyed high spirits. The Group began to attract international attention, but was still virtually ignored by other than the Negro press in the United States.

The P-51C's were gradually being replaced by D's, and to the man, they believed that nothing could approach the Mustang's performance. Captain Edward "Topper" Toppins of the 99th scored three of his four victories in a C. "Having flown the P-40 during most of my tour, it was a great thrill to fly a ship which gave me such an overwhelming mastery of the engagement." Lieutenant Robert W. Williams of the 100th had similar feelings regarding "Duchess Arlene," his Mustang: "It was the finest conventional airplane ever made, and I can whip anyone who says it isn't."

Captain Freddie Hutchins of the 302nd will always have kind words for "Little Freddie," one of six P-51C's he flew in combat. He was forced to make a crash landing in an area heavy with trees. Both wings and tail section were ripped off, with Freddie coming to rest with little more than a seat beneath him, and a stick in his hand. Hutchins exclaimed, "I had a scratch over my left eye, and little more to show for it."

Then there was old Thurston "Go pee up a rope" Gaines whose rather original nickname was acquired resultant from his favorite phrase when annoyed by a squadron mate. Lieutenant Gaines nearly extended his P-51D beyond its capabilities. He was going to land his Mustang out of a loop, with wingtanks filled to capacity, no less. He flew down over the runway at a pretty good clip, pulled up into a beautiful loop, but misjudged his distance by a couple of feet. He hit the ground with such force as to dislodge both wing tanks which slid down the runway. He bent the gear rather badly, and incurred the wrath of Colonel Davis who immediately grounded him, but not before fining him $300 for his efforts.

Colonel Davis, in his year-end message to his men, told them: "I cannot fail to mention the all-important fact that your achievements have been recognized. Unofficially you are known by an untold number of bomber crews as those who can be depended upon, and whose appearance means certain protection from enemy fighters. The bomber crews have told others of your accomplishments, and your good reputation has preceded you in many parts where you may think you are unknown. The Commanding General of Fifteenth Fighter Command has stated that we are doing a good job and thus, the official report of our operations is a creditable one."

The 332nd's missions with the Fifteenth Air Force had its climax on March 24, 1945 when, with Colonel Davis leading, the group flew cover for B-17's in a 1,600-mile round trip attack on Berlin, the longest mission in the Fifteenth Air Force's history. Three other Mustang Groups, the 31st, 52nd, and 325th, also participated with a P-38 unit, the First Fighter Group. The pilots of the 332nd were briefed to relieve the 1st FG at 11 o'clock over Brux, and carry the bombers to the outskirts of Berlin. At that point, the 31st was to take over. Upon arrival at the relief point, however, the 31st was late, and the 332nd was instructed to continue over the target. Just before reaching the target, Colonel Davis' Mustang, "Bennie," developed engine trouble, and he was forced to turn back. Captain Armour G. McDaniel took over command.

Over the target, the Group encountered several German jet propelled fighters, Me-262's. Up to this point, only two confirmed victories over the vaunted 262 had been scored by XV Fighter Command, both by the 31st, and on this date, the 332nd scored three of eight confirmations, the other five again going to the 31st.

In the first victory for the Red Tails, 1st Lieutenant Roscoe Browne started an attack only to find one of the jets hanging onto his tail. Maneuverability of the Mustang and evasive tactics saved Browne. Weaving first left, then right, caused the enemy fighter to overshoot him. Now on the tail of the jet, Browne closed and fired several bursts into the Messerschmitt. The pilot parachuted to safety while his jet spun into the ground.

Flight Officer Charles V. Brantley didn't know it when he scored his victory, the second 262 for the 332nd. Firing on his adversary, he saw strikes on the fuselage, but as he closed in for more shots, the jet nosed over and Brantley passed over him. Other pilots told of seeing the 262 continue the dive to crash into the ground.

The remaining victory confirmed that day was scored by 1st Lieutenant Earle R. Lane, when he followed a jet in a dive that started at 20,000 feet and ended at 6,000 with Lane firing repeated short bursts that set the jet afire. Fellow pilots described the 262 as belching black smoke and out of control as it continued screaming toward the ground. Group leader, Captain McDaniel and Lieutenant Leon Spears were shot down and became prisoners of war, Lieutenant Hannibal Cox, a daring pilot, had 1 foot of his wing shot off but returned to complete 65 missions. For successfully escorting the bombers, outstanding and agressive combat technique, the Group was awarded the DISTINGUISHED UNIT CITATION.

On March 31, the Red Tails completed another outstanding mission. On that day, while strafing near Linz, Austria, they encountered 17 Messerschmitts and Focke-Wulfs. In a wild dogfight the Group successfully shot down 13 with three probables, and one damaged, without loss to themselves. Lieutenant Robert W. Williams, who was credited with two victories, related: "I dived into a group of enemy aircraft. After getting on the tail of one, I gave him a few short bursts. My fire hit the mark and the enemy plane fell off and tumbled into the ground. On pulling away from my victim, I found another Jerry on my tail. To evade his guns I made a steep turn. Just as I had turned another plane shot across in front of my ship. Immediately I began firing on him. The plane went into a steep dive and later crashed."

The next day, April 1, in the Wels, Austria area, the 332nd destroyed 12 more planes, bringing the two-day total to 25 air victories. On April 26, the Group concluded its combat career destroying the last four enemy aircraft in the Mediterranean Theater of Operations before the end of the war. The Group concluded 14 months' operations with its 311th mission flown on April 30, 1945. Hostilities ceased at midnight May the 8th.

On September 30, three squadrons of the 332nd boarded the S.S. Levi Woodbury, and arrived at the New York Port of Embarkation on October 16. The fourth squadron (the 302nd) had been disbanded on March 7. The remaining squadrons were deactivated at Camp Kilmer, New Jersey, and once again the men were sent back to Tuskegee, with some heading for Godman Field, Kentucky, the recently designated home base for the all Negro 477th Composite Group.

The conditions existing at Tuskegee Army Air Field were even more deplorable than in 1943 when the vast majority of trainees were shipped out. To date, no substantial substitutions of white by black personnel were made, though there were many Negroes qualified for each position at the field. With the large influx of war veterans, Negro officers for the most part were relegated to positions that gave them little chance for promotion. While they were denied equal opportunities for advancement, they witnessed rapid advancement of young white officers with limited experience who were often less qualified.

The tension over the discriminatory practices at Tuskegee received publicity when a series of articles published by the Pittsburgh Courier related the "Inside Story of Tuskegee." The Negroes filled the positions of "assistants." There was an assistant to the assistant Mess Officer, assistant to the assistant Supply

Officer, and even assistants to a makeshift position as Post Beautification Officer. It was humiliating. Hundreds of able-bodied men were sitting around Tuskegee doing practically nothing. Even Lieutenant Colonel George S. Roberts, former Commander of both the 99th and 332nd, met with the same degrading treatment. He was assigned as Bachelor Officer Quarters Officer, a position that the lowest non-com could have held. Of course, such an assignment would have been considered an insult to a white officer of equal experience and rank. It was evident that the Air Corps had no place for Negro war veterans, and over 100 holders of the Distinguished Flying Cross, as well as hundreds of experienced ground personnel could find no hope for a military future.

During 1944 and '45, TAAF had become the catch-all for every Negro program in the Air Corps. Within a radius of five miles, not only the increase in numbers of men but also the variety of activities caused administrative and training problems there. At times, portions of the field were under the Third Air Force, the Air Service Command, the Technical Training Command, and the Flying Training Command, most of which had little knowledge of the variety of activities supervised by other commands through the one small post headquarters. The field was training Negro pre-aviation cadets, preflight pilots, preflight bombardier-navigators, preflight bombardiers, basic pilots, advanced single-engine pilots, advanced twin-engine pilots, and pilots in transitional training in the P-40's after graduation. The field also trained field artillery liaison pilots for the ground forces and Haitian and French colonial cadets. It also acted as a pool, holding enlisted and officer specialists awaiting assignment. Now the veterans were returning en masse. It is doubtful that any more chaotic conditions, outside the war zone, ever existed at a U.S. Army Air Corps base.

In a letter to the War Department in late 1945, President Patterson of Tuskegee Institute, who had been so instrumental in activating the Negro program, suggested that TAAF be closed. The laws of segregation were causing problems far out of proportion to the results now being achieved. The mass discontent and displeasure from both the military and civilian population, as well as the monumental expenses being incurred could not continue without grave consequences.

On June 21, 1945, Colonel Benjamin Davis had assumed command of the 477th Composite Group. This unit consisted of two medium bombardment squadrons, the 616th and 617th, originally components of the now defunct 477th Bombardment Group Medium, and two fighter squadrons from the 332nd Fighter Group, the 99th and 100th. Returning veterans who were allowed to remain in the service were rapidly transferred to Godman Field, as space allowed, and by January 1946, Tuskegee Army Air Field was virtually closed.

The 99th Combat Days

P-40s of the 99th line up for take-off. Foggia, Italy, 1944. Note wing riders to guide pilot.

ALL-NEGRO U.S. FIGHTER PLANE SQUADRON. Ground crew members of a U.S. fighter squadron based in North Africa work on the engine and landing gear of one of the P-40 Warhawk fighter planes used by the squadron. In the foreground stands a 500-pound bomb.

ALL-NEGRO U.S. FIGHTER PLANE SQUADRON. Ground crew members servicing a P-40 War-hawk, American fighter plane, pause in their duties to watch another Warhawk piloted by a mem-ber of 99ths fighter squadron glide in for a landing upon returning from a mission. The scene took place at an airfield in Tunisia, Africa, where the fighter squadron is based. The squadron was trained in the U.S. and has seen action in the Allied aerial offensive which preceded landings n Sicily.

P-40L Warhawk of the 99th Fighter Squadron. Note tricolor Marking on Vertical fin. At this time squadron was assigned to the 79th Fighter Group, under Colonel Earl Bates.

Mechanics of the 99th ready a Merlin powered P-40L. Line Chief of the 99th at this time was Mast. Sgt. Ellsworth Dansby.

The ground crew of the 99th Fighter Squadron, gasses up a Curtiss P-40 in preparation for mission. Termoli, Italy, 20 December 1943.

99th FS P-40L "NONA II" bellied in with loss of port wing after completing mission thoug damaged on take-off.

78

2nd Lt. John L. Hamilton, the first member of the 99th to receive the Purple Heart.

ALL-NEGRO U.S. FIGHTER PLANE SQUADRON. Guns mounted on P-40 Warhawk fighter planes are cleaned and repaired by ground crew members of the squadron.

Maj. Gen. John K. Cannon, commander 12th USAAF, congratulates Capt. C.B. Hall, Brazil, IND., who shot down two German planes over bridge head south of Rome. Hall flies with 99th Negro Fighter Squadron which knocked down 12 German fighters in 2 days. Capt. L.R. Curtis, Hartford, Conn., and Lt. W. V. Eagleson, Bloomington, Inc., (background) each got one.

Captain Charles B. Hall, the first Negro member of the Army Air Corps to down an enemy aircraft. The date, July 2, 1943, the aircraft, a Focke-Wulf 190.

80

99th Fighter pilot, 1st Lt. Robert W. Diez, of Portland Oregon, shot down an FW-190 on 27 Jan., 1944, and another the next day. Note RAF flight jacket.

Major George "Spanky" Roberts, Commander, and members of the 99th Fighter Squadron. Top row, L to R: Heber Houston, William Alsbrook, Wilson Eagleson, Charles Bailey, Albert Manning, "Spanky" Alva Temple, George Greay, Clarance Dart, Herman "Ace" Lawson, Bill Campbell, Edward Thomas. Kneeling: L to Rt: Charles Jamerson, Charles Tate, "Herky" Perry, and Leonard "Black" Jackson.

Lt. Charles Tate models typical flight gear worn by the 99th.

Lt. Charles Tate, and P-51C Mustang. The 99th began flying Mustangs after being attached to the 332nd FG in July, 1944 at Ramitelli, Italy.

P-51C Mustangs of the 99th FS, 332nd FG. Ramitelli, Italy, August, 1944.

Capt. Ed Toppins, and his TOPPER III. Toppins confirmed 4 victories during his tour with the 99th.

S/Sgt. Wm. McCoo o Salem, N.J., crew chief be lieves in taking care of hi P-51.

Mustangs of the 99th FS, line up prior to take-off. Checkerboard nose band in dark blue and white, with "A" designation, characterized the 99th.

Lt. Alphonso Davis of the 99th FS.

P-51 of the 99th taxies to take-off position.

Lt. Edward Thomas of Chicago, Ill., and his crew chief.

"APACHE II" P-51C
99th FS, Ramitelli, It

1C, "Knobby" heads
vn steel mat for take-
B-24 tail gun posi-
seen at right.

O.K. for take-off signal given, as pilot pours the coal to his Mustang.

P-39Q Airacobra, flown by the 332nd while stationed near Naples at Capodochina, attached to the 12th Air Force.

The 332nd Fighter Group

Group Commanders of the four Mustang Fighter Groups of the 306th Fighter Wing. Top to Bottom: the 31st, 52nd,, 332nd, and 325th.

Refueling a 51D Mustang.

P-51Cs and Ds, of the 100th Fighter Squadron.

Engine removal and installation. Time: 10 hours.

Refueling Wing tank, P-51D.

90

t Lt. Henry Bowman, Armament Officer of the 100th Fighter Squadron, and crew chief S/Sgt.
bb, and Armorer Cpt. W. C. Clark check 50 Calibers on P-51C.

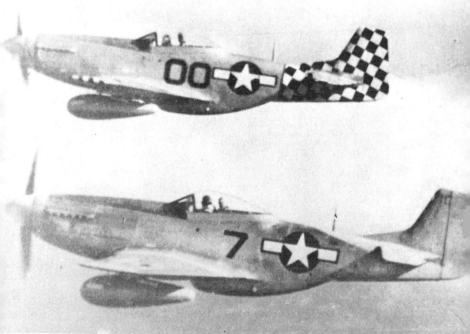

e 325th, and the 332nd. Checkertail Mustang flown by Colonel Ernie Beverly, CO of the
5th. No. 7, flown by Colonel Davis, CO, 332nd.

Colonel Benjamin O. Dav
in cockpit of P-51C, "E
Request". At left is Ca
tain Nelson Brooks, in ce
ter is Lt. Bill Thompso

Colonel Benjamin Davis, (2nd from left) and Captain Andrew D. "Jug" Turner, squadron lea
100th Fighter Squadron (far right) confer with command of the 306th Fighter Wing, of wh
the 332nd was part.

100th FS Mustangs roll out of revetment area and head for take off.

S/Sgt. William Pitts, (center with cap) and fellow mechanics check out 100th FS Mustang.

Line Chief M/Sgt. Nathaniel Wade, who succeeded M/Sgt James Jones, shown in front of P51C, 100th F.S.

Colonel Benjamin O. Davis, Jr., CO, 332nd FG, and Capt. Andrew D. "Jug" Turner, Squadron Leader, 100th FS. Mustang in background exhibits markings on vertical fin of the four Mustang Groups of the 306th Fighter Wing, the 31st, 52nd, 325th, and 332nd.

Captain Richard Caesar, Engineering Officer of the 100th FS instructs his men who are readying "Hammerin' Hank", P-51C of Lt. Bob Nelson.

Checking the fuel supply.

Mustang Art. P-51D of Lt. Charles White, 301st FS.

P-51C being made ready.

Lt. Willard Woods, and "We Three" of the 100th FS. Crew Chief on wing.

P-51C, "Nuff Stuff", 332nd FG.

Lt. Carol Woods, tells it all to his Crew Chief, and Armourer.

Mustangs of the 332nd.

100th FS, P-51D.

1st Lt. John Briggs, St. Louis, Mo., and P-51, "Travelin' Lite". 100th FS.

T/Sgt. Charles Haynes, and S/Sgt. James Sheppard, along with M/Sgt. Frank Bradley install wing tank, 100th FS.

Capt. Armour McDaniel inspects flack damage to his Mustang incurred during a straffing missio along the Danube. L to R, S/Sgt. Richard Adams, McDaniel, Lt. James McFatridge, and Lt. Uly ses Taylor.

"Target for Today", Group Operations officer, Capt. Edward C. Gleed.

Captain Roy Spencer, his crew chief and armorer. All of the 302nd FS, 332nd FG. "Toleka III" named for his wife.

Group Briefing, 332nd FG, Italy, 1944.

S/Sgt. James E. Johnso[n] sheet metal worker of th[e] 100th applies skillfull har[d] in lettering "Bernice Baby[."] The name Bernice is th[at] of his wife, and also th[at] of the pilot of this pa[r]ticular aircraft, Lt. Ja[ck] Holsclaw.

Captain Edward C. Gleed,
CO of the 302nd FS, and
later Group Operations Officers of the 332nd. Mus-
tang "Lucifer Jr."

Group briefing, all four squadrons of the 332nd.

Pfc. John T. Fields, armorer of the 100th FS.

Crew Chiefs of the 100th FS waiting for the squadron to return from mission.

Captain "Luke" Weathers of the 302nd FS, (on Wing 2nd from left) and the crew chiefs of the 302nd. Sgts., Eli, Riddley, Johnson, Blevins, Lightfoot, Farr, Teamer, Strothers, Jacobs, Johnson, Tuttle, and Thomas. All are members of "A" Flight.

Captain Fred Hutchins, 302nd FS.

Lt. Charles McGee, and his crew chief, of the 302nd FS, 332nd FG.

Captain Andrew D. Turner, CO of the 100th FS, and Lt. Clarence D. "Lucky" Lester of the 100th. Lester has three enemy aircraft to his credit. All knocked down on one mission.

t. Robert W. Williams,
00th FS.

Men of the 100th FS, L to R, Lt. Dempsey Morgan, Lt. Carroll Woods, Lt. Bob Nelson, Captain
Andrew Turner, CO, and Lt. "Lucky" Lester. Mustang "Skippers Darlin' " belongs to Turner.

Captain William T. Mattison, Operations Officers 100th FS, and his crew chief, S/Sgt. Alfred D. Morris.

Colonel Benjamin O. Davis Jr., CO 332nd FG, and his P-47D Thunderbolt. The 332nd flew P-47s for about a month before converting to Mustangs.

Lts. John Briggs & Spurgeon Ellington.

Captains Jack Holsclaw, Lowell Steward, and Clarence Lester, all of the 100th FS.

Lt. "Lucky" Lester, and his crew chief enjoy a moment of relaxation.

Lts. John Briggs and Willard Woods.

Lt. Spurgeon Ellington, and his P-51 D, "Lollipoops II", named for his wife Maria.

The 100th FS, Purnell Goodenough, Lowell C. Steward, and "Dopey" Hall.

Captain Andrew D. Turner, OK for take off.

Brigadier General Benjamin O. Davis Sr., presents Silver Star to his son, Col. B. O. Davis Jr., and DFCs to Captain Joseph Elsberry, Lts. Jack Holsclaw, and "Lucky" Lester.

Captain Wendell O. Pruitt, and Crew Chief, S/Sgt. Sam Jacobs with their Mustang, "Alice-Jo" Pruitt was credited with three enemy aircraft, and was awarded the DFC for his part in sinking a German destroyer with machine gun fire. They are members of the 302nd FS.

1st. Lt. Lee "Buddy" Archer, of the 302nd, his crew chief, S/Sgt. Blevins, and his Mustang, "Ina, The Macon Belle".

Lt. Lee A. "Buddy" Archer of the 302nd, teamed with Wendell Pruitt to become the heaviest 1-2 punch of the 332nd FG.

Captain Wendell O. Pruitt of the 302nd, called by his CO, the best damn pilot in the outfit.

Flight Officer Charles Brantley, St. Louis, Mo. was credited on March 24, 1945, with one of three Me-262 jets destroyed by the 332nd on 1600 mile round trip mission to Berlin.

S/Sgt. William Pitts, and fellow mechanic ready Mustang.

100th FS, prior to take-off.

100th FS, ready for take-off.

P-51s of the 100th FS, buzz the tower, Ramitelli, Italy, 1944.

B-24 Liberator, shown during the bombing of Ploesti oil fields in Rumania. The 332nd flew escort for many of the Ploesti missions.

1st. Lt. Robert W. Williams, just returned from victorious mission of March 31, 1945, during which he was credited with two FW-190s. (Williams is 5th from right, also seen below)

P-51D "Duchess Arlene" belongs to Lt. Robert W. Williams of the 100th.

Flight Surgeons of the 332nd Fighter Group. L to R, Major Vance Marchbanks, Chief Surgeon, and Capts. William K. Allen, Arnold Moloney, and Bascomb Waugh.

The 477th Bombardment Group
477th Composite Group
332nd Fighter Wing

Another of the late Judge William H. Haste's demands began to develop. (Note: During the compiling of this material, it was brought to our attention that Judge William H. Hastie, Senior U.S. Circuit Judge, has died in Philadelphia, Pa.) It must be remembered that Judge Hastie, formerly the Civilian Aide on Negro Affairs, under Secretary of War Henry L. Stimson, had resigned as a protest to the Armys failure in most cases to train Negroes for any other than the most menial of tasks. Finally, by mid 1943, Negro candidates were being screened to determine their relative aptitude as pilots for multi-engine usage, bombardiers, and navigators, though to date no real plans had been made for their usage. Class 43J was the first class at Tuskegee with about half of its members training in the multi-engine Beechcraft AT-10, for future use in expectation that the bomb group program would develop. Major Clay Albright was selected to head the new twin-engine school, with Lt. Milton "Baby" Hall of Owensboro, Ky., a member of class 42K, assisting him in an administrative capacity. Instructors of the newly formed school were 1st Lt. Leonard B. Crozier, and 2nd Lt. Robert B. Meagher. The plan being that pilots for twin-engine training were to be selected from the Basic class of cadets, and scheduled to receive 70 hours of advanced flying at Tuskegee in the Beechcraft, with actual bomber pilot training to be conducted elsewhere. Instructors from Turner Field, Ga. were now attached to TAAF to familiarize the Tuskegee based mechanics in the fundamentals of the AT-10.

It might be interesting to note at this time that on September 30, 1943, the first class of field artillery officers trained as liaison pilots at Tuskegee AAF received their wings. Colonel Noel F. Parrish presented the fifteen men with letters of appointment and commended them on their ability to master the primary stage of flying in the nine weeks of intensive training. 1st Lt. Charles T. Hood presented the men with their liaison wings, representing Capt. Errol W. Bechtold, director of training. The graduated officers reported to Fort Sill, Oklahoma for advanced and tactical training. The future of these men was rather obscure however, and the Army was quite successful in limiting their training and usage for further duty.

Because Tuskegee was officially classified under the Advanced Training Wing of the Training Command, directives concerning the preflight schools sometimes never reached it, with the result that training there was often out of step with that at other stations. One advantage of the compact school was that all previous records of a particular cadet were always available, but one of the disadvantages of the concentration of training at the field is trouble in the traffic pattern resulting from the various speeds and types of planes. Periods of crowding, followed by slack periods were normal at the station. In late 1943 when the question of superimposing the bombardier-navigator program upon existing activities came up, the station was already complaining of excess men, for who no assignments existed, with the number increasing rapidly.

Tuskegee informed the Air Corps that for the past six months, enlisted men had been sent to the station from technical schools of both the Air Corps and the Signal Corps, classified and trained in jobs for which in the main, there were no positions at the station. No further training could be given the men as they were all specialists, and in most cases due to their rank were not suitable for reclassification nor for assignment to any other job on the station. This was certainly a waste of manpower and malassignment of personnel, and a serious imposition on TAAF. Many of these men were technical trainees for use in the bombardment group, which to date was only a questionable paper proposal. To complicate matters, the addition of bombardier and navigator trainees to the total picture would have been intolerable.

The Air Forces decided to schedule a few trainee classes into existing schools formerly used for white trainees only, some being located in areas previously thought of as impossible for training Negroes. Staff Sgt. William Pitts (later assigned to duty as a mechanic with the 100th FS) recalls the reception he and seven other trainees from Tuskegee received upon arriving for basic mechanic training, a six month course at the Air Corps School, Lincoln, Nebraska. "We arrived by train in Lincoln, and nobody, from the commander of the school, to the other Negro GIs station there as orderlys, and mess attendants would believe we were to be trained as mechanics. There was never a provision for this type of training in the Air Corps manual, and no one could understand that it had come to pass. Several days went by as they isolated us off by ourselves without being sure of just what action to take. Our orders meant nothing." It was not uncommon to hear, "Hell, whats wrong with headquarters, making a mistake like this, sending all these niggers for mechanic training when we all know there ain't no nigger air force.!" However, upon completing the six month course under a Captain Fox, who was assigned as their C.O., the men graduated with the highest record ever achieved at the basic school at Lincoln, and went on to the advanced training center at Buffalo, N.Y.

The first class of navigation cadets, selected in part from men eliminated from the Tuskegee fighter program, arrived at Hondo Field, Texas on October 25, 1943, for cadet navigation training, although a definite decision on the bombardment unit still had not yet been made. Since the activation of this unit was involved with the outcome of discussions on the future of Negro combat units then under way, hesitancy about continuing plans for the new bombardment group increased within Air Corps headquarters. In some conferences and communications the group was definitely mentioned as being "out", in others, planning for the group went ahead. "We must have a decision, a definite one soon." stated Brigadier General Mervin E. Gross. The training schedule then being followed for Tuskegee would provide more pilots than could be used by the fighter group. If the bomber group was to be discontinued, no directive eliminating it had been given to the responsible chiefs of staff. If it was to be continued, the First Air Force had to be directed to prepare to receive its personnel and activate its units. If the group was not to be activated, the Air Operations, Commitments, and Requirements and the Air Training Divisions should be informed so that other uses of personnel earmarked for it could be made, otherwise, the Air Corps would find it difficult to explain why it had trained so many men for whom it had no need.

General Arnold, in the spring of 1943 had reacted to the suggestion of the Tuskegee commander that political pressures might force a change in the Air Forces' training program. He remarked that the training program would be determined by him in the future as it had been in the past, and that it would be based only upon the foreseeable use of Negro squadrons. On October 27, he decided to go ahead with the bombardment group. He directed that it be organized, trained, equipped, and sent to North Africa, to join the 99th Fighter Squadron. It would now be necessary to set up auxiliary supporting service units as well, General Gross advised.

Although Air Training had warned of their needs as far back as July, it now appeared that there would be insufficient pilots to activate the replacement training unit for the medium bomb group in December as planned. Delays of this type were to play a continuing part in the career of the new 477th Bombardment Group. Demands on Tuskegee for single-engine pilots continued to grow in order to meet the needs of the 332nd FG and the 99th FS. As schedules for twin-engine training were trimmed and altered to fill these demands, one or another phase of the supply of men to the bombardment group went out of kilter, and the group itself was continually blamed for these difficulties inherited from Air Corps indecision.

The Air Training Division requested that Tuskegee be relieved of the responsibility of producing all types of Negro pilots because its production rate was not sufficient to meet replacement fighter requirements and, at the same time, turn out enough pilots to meet Operation Day requirements for the bombardment group. Restriction of the maximum production possible at Tuskegee, Air Training predicted, would mean a delay in the bomb group until July 1945. Excess Negro flying cadets could possibly be entered in existing white schools, thus increasing the output of Negro pilots. Instead of acquiecing or increasing facilities at Tuskegee and entering the pilots in white schools, headquarters Army Air Forces, rescinded the requirements for the bomb group on November 15. With the exception of B-25 transition, all pilot training continued at Tuskegee, with successive O-Days set for the bomb group, until it was reached on January 10, 1945. Navigators alone were trained elsewhere, the first class graduating on February 26, 1944, thus becoming the first air cadets to train outside of Tuskegee. By the time four classes had entered, with two of them graduating, Hondo Field had some observations to make about the Negro program: The morale of the Negro cadets is as high as that of any group at the field. Instructors reported almost no complaining or fault finding on their part and restrictions and additional study classes imposed upon them were equally accorded to white classes with no loss of sense of humor or efficiency among the men. Colored cadets fly missions prescribed by the standard details of the missions. White pilots fly the planes. In general there had been but few cases of animosity toward Negro cadets from white cadets, and in many instances athletic competition between the groups was exhibited. The colored cadets lived in their own barracks, and had their own classrooms. They ate in the same mess, and were extended the same privileges, though on a segregated basis.

In the meantime, an imbalance in the production of pilots and aircrewmen, followed by a shortage of trainees continued. By the spring of 1944, Tuskegee noted that the balance in production in pilots, bombardiers, and navigators was going askew. While Tuskegee was turning out classes of 7 to 15 twin-engine pilots, classes of 20 to 87 preflight bombardiers and navigators were leaving the school for advanced training, resulting in applications for flying training from men in the Ground and Service Forces being discontinued. The result of this chaos as originally predicted by Air Training, was that the 477th was not fully manned with pilots and aircrewmen until the summer of 1945.

Meanwhile the men of the 332nd FG, now in transition and combat training at Selfridge Field, Mich, became aware that multi-engine training was planned, and the option was open for some of the fighter jocks of larger stature. Those around six feet, and approximately 200 lbs. plus, with flying gear felt that the new phase of flying might insure their future use as combat pilots, as the P-40s and 39s being used, were not designed with them in mind. Among this initial group to become involved in the multi-engine program were: Lts. George Knox, Charles Stanton, C.I. Williams, Peter Verwayne, Jim Mason, Bill Ellis, and Daniel "Chappie" James, to mention a few.

Mather Field, Calif., was the site of the transitional training, and the men moved immediately into B-25s, with no intermediate training aircraft. After approximately 100 hours in the Mitchells, the men returned to Selfridge Field, and began being complemented by men graduating from the multi-engine classes at Tuskegee. To date the group still had not yet been formed, and the men were under the command of Wyoming born West-Pointer, Colonel Robert R. Selway, who also had commanded the 332nd at Selfridge. By the time the group was officially activated on January 15, 1944, the 332nd, with Col. Davis, already had left for Italy. At Selfridge, instruction continued, and in all cases, was handled by "qualified" white personnel. However, in many cases, this was not the case, and in one particular instance, 2nd Lt. Haldane King was being shown the finer points of the B-25, when he learned that his instructor had 27 less hours in the ship than did he. Needless to say, anamosity was built up in some cases, and several incidents, racial in nature did occur. It became generally felt that the white instructors were in many cases using the 477th as a stepping stone for speedy promotion, and many of them were relegated to instruction of the Negro crews to sharpen their own inadequacies. Another problem became evident in that not one of the Negro officers were allowed residence on the base. Many of the officers homes were allowed to remain vacant rather than house the Negroes. The base commander stated that, "All of the Negro personnel were designated as trainees, and thus were not entitled to such priviliges, which were extended to supervisors and instructors." This philosophy, and these designations were to exist as part of Colonel Selway's program throughout his command.

During this period, the administrative staff began moving into Selfridge. The administrative cadre had been selected from men at Tuskegee, some previously in the pilot training program, who were sent to OCS at Miami Beach, Florida, with the option of returning to Tuskegee in an administrative capacity, or joining the newly proposed Bombardment Group. Many jumped at the latter, as it was apparent that Tuskegee was not providing an opportunity for advancement, and the hope of leaving the known for possible greener pastures of the unknown, gave hopes to many. About 16 were picked to staff the 477th. March 15, 1944, was the date scheduled for arrival at Selfridge. Colonel Selway welcomed the men, and told them of the potential awaiting them. Colonel Selway selected the positions to be filled by the non rated personnel as he had done the rated. Again, many were more qualified than their white contemporaries, and in many cases were doing the administration, but received neither rank nor recognition for doing so. Many enlisted personnel were left over from the 332nd, and were transferred to the new group and assigned new duties, but as yet aircraft crews were still not ready, and very few bombardiers and navigators had arrived.

As the ranks grew in number, unrest also grew, as no officer club facilities existed, and had Detroit not been so close, and become known as the "Negroes Mecca", it was felt that greater disturbances would have resulted. When a club was established as an afterthought, its quality left much to be desired, and attendance was minimal. An attempt was made to accommodate the enlisted personnel, as their number was far greater, and they were more limited with regards to freedom of movement. In the mean time, several of the Negro Officers tried to enter the white officers club, a move for which they were repremanded. Word got to General Frank O.D. Hunter, Commander of the 1st Air Force at Mitchell Field, N.Y., which prompted a visit by him to Selfridge. He gathered all of his officers, black and white, after being apprised that 40 to 50 black officers had applied for membership in the club and stated: As long as I am commander of the 1st Air Force, there will be no racial mixing at any post under my command." He further stated, "There is no racial problem on this base, and there will be none." He claimed that outside agitation in Detroit had made his Negroes 'surly'.

Almost simultaneously, Congress appropriated $75,000 to build the Negro officers a club, but before the club was complete, such pressure had been brought to bear that orders had come through to move the 477th to Godman Field, Kentucky, the air field adjoining Fort Knox. The group moved out in the dark of night, the men really not sure as to their destination. The date of their arrival at Godman was May 5, 1944, assuming duty on May the 6th. The selection of Godman as home for the 477th was always steeped with controversy, but as were most orders and decisions involving the black air force, this was no exception. It was generally agreed that the agitation surrounding Selfridge and the Detroit community, with pressures from the press and active civilian organizations greatly contributed to the decision. Though the officers club incident stirred much attention to the problems of the men, it was but one means of venting frustration. Godman, again being rather isolated, it was perhaps hoped to present the same conditions as did Tuskegee. Being away from urbanization, and adjacent to Fort Knox, it was not too difficult to police the men, the MPs and tank battalions at Fort Knox rendering this rather easily, and the area would be free of outside agitation and community influence.

The field was rather small and inadequate for the 477th, and its accompanying material group. The runways were rather short, and though the field was not totally inactive, it had not accommodated so large an operation, and took considerable effort to bring it up to the standards of the day. There had supposedly been a B-26 outfit stationed there with minimum training exercises. The field caused the men to develop quite a proficiency at landing and taking off in a rather short area. The 477th was not allowed to utilize any of the facilities at Fort Knox. Even the theater segregated the black personnel, either to the rear, or on one side or the other, and the PX did not welcome the men. Again minor incidents occurred. All department heads at Godman were white, including the squadron leaders of the four bombardment units. The 616th was commanded by Capt. Gandie, the 617th, Captain Parker, the 618th, Capt. Schreck, and the 619th, Captain Tyson.

The auxiliary flying personnel were arriving in mass now. The bombardier-navigator personnel, having completed their transitional training were now coming to Godman. A problem arose with the aerial gunners. No school was training them, and after five or six received training with a white unit, they began instructing, and trained many of the future Negro candidates to fill these positions. Myrtle Beach, and Walterboro, South Carolina were used for gunnery training (tactical) just as the 332nd had used Oscoda, Mich. The commander at Walterboro, Lt. Col. Sam Triffy, it may be interesting to note, was releaved of his command due to incidents occurring during the stay of the 477th. When the group went on its navigational training flights, Tuskegee, Selfridge, Teterboro, Des Moines and Bolling Field were the only available facilities serving the group. the others initially provided no accommodations for the Negro airmen.

As previously mentioned, Godman's facilities were just too small to adequately handle the group, and on March 15th, the unit moved to Freeman Field, in Seymour, Indiana. Immediately upon arrival, Colonel Selway issued orders dividing the officer's clubs along previously determined lines, supervisors and trainees. Officers Club #1 was the designation for the Negro Club. It had formerly been a non com club, and was referred to by the men as "Uncle Tom's Cabin". The white club was designated as Club #2, and was off limits to other than instructors, or supervisors. It must be remembered that all the black officers, whether medical personnel with several years of experience in their chosen field, administrative officers, or pilots, some with 2½ years experience, were designated as trainees, with the Negroes justifiably complaining that this was still 'Jim Crow' by any other name. General Hunter again issued orders stating that any insubordination would be met by confinement to the guard house. Colonel Selway feared the consequences of such an order, and felt that he was being put in the same spot that Colonel Byrd, former commander at Selfridge had previously experienced, and he had lost command of Selfridge for similar restrictions placed upon the 332nd. Hunter, on March 10, stated: "I'd be delighted for them to commit enough action that I can court martial some of them."

Thus the 477th was a particularly tense organization. The fact that the unit was a promotion mill for whites with no position of responsibility in any flying organization going to a Negro, however qualified, was galling. Add to this the fact that the first contingent of pilots had arrived in January, 1944 and had gone through several repeats of rudimentary training awaiting navigators, and bombardiers, and now continual social pressures, and you have all the ingredients for trouble. The Negro personnel at Freemen were in the majority, 400 officers, and 2500 enlisted men, thus giving them numerical superiority over the 250 white officers and 600 enlisted men, created further frustration. Many disgruntled remarks were made by whites while in the presence of the colored troops, such as, "I'll do everything possible to get transferred out of here." If one of them makes a crack at my wife, so help me, I'll kill him." "They are purposely trying to goof up so they won't have to go overseas." Remarks of similar nature were reported from the colored contingent. It must not be implied that the situation was one sided, but it must be emphacized that the white position was backed up in most cases by the command.

On April 5, 1945, an incident occurred unparalled in Air Corps history. It was on this day that the Combat Training Squadron, the administrative unit of the 477th arrived from Godman to Freeman Field. Though they had not been briefed on General Hunter's order of March 10, it was an acknowledged fact that they were well aware of what was to transpire in the next few days. Colonel Selway had been made aware that some trouble might occur at the officers club #2 that evening, and Selway, the master strategist that he was, ordered the base Provost Marshall, a Major A.M. White (who had been suspended from an Ohio Police Department for killing two blacks), to station men at the front door of the club, and to lock all other doors to prevent entry by Negroes. The Negro officers were well aware of what they were doing, and had several strategy meetings on how not to create a distasteful situation, and how to prevent it. The main problem they had for quite some time prior to this was keeping the enlisted men from getting involved, they being very volatile and hostile toward the system, and ready to strike back against their white supervisors on the spur of the moment. The officer's calmer heads prevailed however, and the enlisted men were quieted down. The philosophy being that an officer could neither be railroaded nor courtmartialed as easily as an enlisted man.

The men involved in the following events had not intended on being arrested for what was to transpire. They had planned on doing everything by the book, to bring attention to their predicament in a totally peaceful manner. Arrest had not been considered. At about 9:15 PM, groups of two and three Negro officers began to arrive at Club #2, and were politely declined admission. The men were in full dress, themselves being cordial and polite, and accepted their refusal very gentlemanly. At about 9:45 PM, Lts. Marsden Thompson, and Shirley Clinton arrived at the club and requested admission. With them were about three other officers, with about 15 or 16 waiting several yards behind. Lt. Thompson was refused admission, but politely stated he would like to utilize his privilege as an officer of the United States Army Air Corps, and enter the club for a drink. He brushed past the officer on duty, and all of the men entered. Later that evening, Lt. Roger Terry used similar tactics to gain entrance, and throughout the next day similar incidents occurred. Within 24 hours, 61 men were arrested, but after four days, only the aforementioned three were held. On April 9th, Colonel Selway called all Negro officers in and ordered them to sign a statement that they understood his regulation dictating club segregation, and in all, 101 Negro officers refused to sign, though 8 did. On April 13, this group was sent to Godman Field via C-47s, and were placed under arrest. Selway now was assured that the "Bad Apples" had been removed, but surprisingly was told on that same day that, approximately 100% of the Negro officers were about to enter the white club, and Selway immediately closed the club. For the first time Selway became genuinely alarmed, and became insightful enough to recognize the real nature of his problem. He called General Hunter, who stated, "We'll just have to use discipline in this matter." He asked: "Are the Negroes very far out of line?" Selway replied, "No sir, they salute and use the right words, but its like somebody with a sneer on their faces, you know after all, these soldiers have to take orders from these young white boys, and they're human beings..."

On April 19, with the approval of General George Marshall, the 101 non-signers were released, only the original Freeman Field three being held. General Hunter was furious. Upon instructions from the War Department, the McCloy Committee was set up to investigate illegal segregation in the Army, and proved that Army Regulation 210-10 prevented the commander from excluding men from entry into an officers club on racial grounds, which the trainer, trainee basis, definitely was. This decision rendered on June 4, 1945, resulted in Colonel Robert Selway being fired as commander of the 477th because of mishandling the unit, and having been faced with a mutiny of black officers. One of General Hunters many comments was: "Was this McCloy Committee composed of Negroes?" As later recalled by Marsden Thompson, one of the Freeman three, "I figure the only reason we were held and tried was because Clinton and I were the first through the door that Major White wrote up." Later reports indicate that Terry, the third, was included because of all the men arrested, he was the only one who forced his way into the club. As it turned out, he was fined $150.00, the only penalty arising from the incident. During the rather lengthy trial, Major White, the Provost Marshall, and his assistant Lt. J.D. Rogers, repeatedly became flustered and confused in their statements, and though they tried to refer to the segregation being based strictly on instructor vs. trainee, rather than black & white, many times were tripped up into admitting otherwise. Colonel Selway was continually admonished by the court martial board for his hostile and arrogant behavior. His attitude and demeanor was disgusting. He continually blamed the former commanders for establishing policy on which he only followed through. The court martial board, composed of Capt. George Knox as president, replacing Colonel B.O. Davis, Capts. Fitzroy Newsom, James Wiley, W.T. Yates, and 1st Lt. William Ming of Chicago as legal council, were all selected by General Hunter because he was so sure of conviction, that he didn't want the "liberals" to say the trial was weighted against the men.

Following the decision, Colonel Selway and his staff remained at Freeman Field in a nominal command status, and Colonel Benjamin O. Davis Jr. assumed command of the 477th, now designated as a Composite group, with the deactivation of the 616th, and 619th Bombardment Squadron, and the contemplated attachment of the 99th Fighter Squadron. The assumption of this command was June 24th, 1945. On July 1st, Colonel Davis assumed command of Godman Field, thus another first in Army history. He selected his staff, and for the first time, all responsible positions were held by Negroes. Major Edward Gleed, former squadron leader of the 302nd FS, and Operations officer of the 332nd FG, became Group Operations Officer, Captain John Beverly, Group Intelligence Officer, Major Andrew "Jug" Turner, former CO of the 100th FS, Deputy Group Commander, and Major Vance H. Marchbanks Jr., Base Surgeon, to mention but a few. Captain C.I. Williams commanded the 617th Bomb Squadron, Captain Elmore Kennedy, the 618th, With Major William A. Campbell commanding the newly assigned 99th FS, with Capt. Edward Toppins, Senior Flight Leader. Major George W. Webb, commanded the 387th Headquarters and Service Squadron, with Capt. Lott S. Carter, the Training Officer, with Major Lee Rayford, Base Operations. The Composite Group set about undergoing intensive tactical training, as the Pacific Theater of Operations had been selected as their next objective. With the cessation of hostilities, however, many of the men returned to civilian life, and in March 1946, the Composite Group moved to Lockbourne Field, Columbus, Ohio. At this time the 99th was flying P-47Ds, and Ns, the bomber squadrons utilizing B-25H and Js. After only two months at Lockbourne, the Composite Group was deactivated and the 332nd Fighter Group was again reactivated. This meant the loss of all multi-engine units, and the men left the service in masses. A few months later, the Group became the 332nd Fighter Wing, and the pilot force being reduced to about 100, now flew P-47N Thunderbolts exclusively. The ground personnel included some 1700 persons, including a detachment of WAAFS, under the command of 1st Lt. Oleta Crain, of Oklahoma.

Under Colonel Davis' command at Lockbourne were: Major Ed Gleed, Executive Officer; Major William T. Mattison, Director of Operations; Major Tom Money, Director of Personnel; Capt. George Evans, Director of Material; Capt. Carroll Woods, Wing Inspector; Major William A. Campbell, CO Fighter Group; Major George Knox, CO of Maintenance and Supply; Major George Webbe, CO Airbase Group; Major Vance Marchbanks, CO Medical Group; and 1st Lt. Lucius Theus, Statistical Controls Officer.

The unit continued until June 1, 1949, when Congressional action, spearheaded by President Harry S. Truman, integrated the armed forces throughout the world.

Shortly after the closing of TAAF, the former base commander, Colonel Noel F. Parrish, in discussing the success of the flying school, had this to say: "How good were our pilots? How good is any pilot? Our men were good enough to graduate from any flying school in the country, we made sure of that, and working together we proved it. We emphasized that a pilot or a man of whatever color, size, or shape is just as good as he proves himself to be. Men, and pilots, have to be considered as individuals. We have had some of the worst pilots in the world right here, and we have had some of the best. In the first place, they flew and fought as men. They may have been classified as Negroes. They may have had pretty good alibis for being failures if they wanted to use these alibis, or they may have been proud of their group as the only one like it in the world, as they had a right to be. But when the test came they had to fly and fight just as men, Americans against a common enemy.

North American B-25J Mitchell, of the 618 Bomb Squadron Godman, Field, Kentucky.

Cadets LeRoy Gillead, Everett Richardson, and Reginald Freeman at Hondo Field, Texas for navigation training.

Class 45-12 Navigators, graduating at Hondo Field, Texas.

477th
Bomb
Group

Cadets Richard Carter, Everett Richardson, and Thomas Giddings during navigation training at Hondo Field, Texas.

Code Class at Tuskegee Army Air Field.

Aerial Gunners, and Mascot, prior to joining the 477th Bomb Group.

Members of the 477th Bombardment Group at Selfridge Field, Michigan, April 1944. L to R. Lts. Harold Hillery, Sam Lynn, Les Williams, and Daniel "Chappie" James.

Crew of B-25J at Godman Field, Ky, 477th Bomb Group, 619th bomb squdron.

Lena Horne visits the men of the 477th at Godman Field, Ky.

Pre-flight check, Godman
Field, Ky.

Brigadier General Benjamin O. Davis Sr., congratulates his son Colonel Benjamin O. Davis, Jr.,
upon assumption of his command of Godman Field, Ky, July, 1945.

136

MP inspection, Godman Field, Ky., 477th Bomb Group.

B-25 take-off, Walterboro, S. Carolina during training of the 477th Bomb Group. This plane is from the 616th Bomb Squad.

B-25 take-off, Godman, Field, Ky.

B-25J, 477th Bomb. Group.

B-25s, cooling it on the apron, 477th Bomb Group.

Lt. R. A. Bynum at Godman Field.

B-25 Aerial Engineers from TAAF at North American Aircraft Co. School.

The 404th Army Service Force Band. This all WAC band received national honors wherever they appeared. The first all Negro WAC group to do so. Shown in May, 1944.

Flight Engineers (Aircraft Engine Mechanics) Class held at Allison Division of General Motors Corporation, Indianapolis, Indiana.

A Few
of the
Crews
from
the
617th

Pilots of the 477th. Shown here are members of the 617th.

B-25s of the 617th BS, Godman Field, Ky.

L to R: Lts. R. Highbaugh, Sam Lynn, Daniel "Chappie" James, Harvey Pinkney, and Capt. Fitzroy Newsum.

Waist Gunner, shown here in B-3 Cold Weather Flight Gear.

(617BS)(10-2-44-146)(B 25 J)(GF KY)

B-25J of the 617th BS, Godman Field, Kentucky.

Best Wishes
Vwomana
Mitch Higginbotham
B-25 Pilot
617th Sq.

Preparing a B-25J.

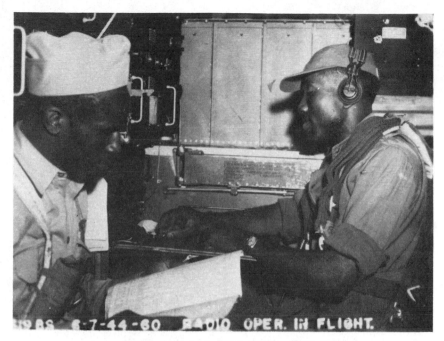

Radio Operator in flight. Godman Field, Ky.

The 619th BS.

Lt. Herky Perry briefs the group prior to take off. Members of the 477th shown here are: seated L to R: Lt. Toler, Capt. C. Jamison, Lt. Wm. Ellis, Lt. John Briggs, Capt. Joe Ellsberry. Standing L to R: Lt. Bynum, Lt. Blue, and Lt. Weldon Groves, seated rear. Photo taken maneuvers at Blythe, Calif., 1946.

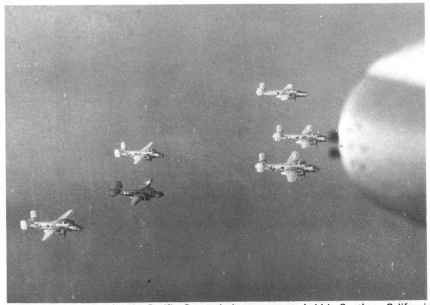

B-25s of the 477th over the Pacific Ocean during war games held in Southern California during 1946. Group was stationed at Blythe, Calif.

On the Flight Line at Blythe, Calif., L to R. Major Andrew "Jug" Turner, Deputy Commander, Capt. Spann Watson (back to camera), Major William Campbell, Commander of the 99th FS, and Captain Fitzroy "Buck" Newsum of the 617th Bombardment Squadron.

1st Lt. John "Mr. Death" Whitehead, of the post war 332nd FW, 100th F.S.

Capt. Elwood T. Driver, CO of the 100t at Lockbourne.

The 332nd Fighter Wing

On the line. In background can be seen P-47N Thunderbolts of the 332nd FW.

Captain Claude Govan briefs the 100th prior to cross country flight.

embers of the 100th FS leave operations for the flight line. Lockbourne Air Force Base, Colum-
s, Ohio.

Tuskegee Airmen Achieving Command Rank in Today's Air Force

General Daniel (Chappie) James, Jr., is Commander in Chief, North American Air Defense Command (NORAD), a bi-national military command consisting of United States and Canadian air defense forces. He also serves as Commander in Chief, United States Air Force Aerospace Defense Command (ADCOM), the United States element of NORAD.

Lieutenant General Benjamin O. Davis Jr., USAF (ret). Graduate of West Point in 1936, General Davis received his pilots wings as a member of the first graduating class at Tuskegee n March 1942. He distinguished himself as commander of the 99th FS, 332nd FG, and the 77th Composite Group. He also became the first black man to command an Army Air Base, his being Godman Field, Ky. and later Lockbourne Field, Ohio. Following duty in Korea, General Davis was assigned as chief of staff for the United Nations Command and U.S. Forces n Korea. He later assumed command of the Thirteenth Air Force in August 1967. After duty s commander in chief, Middle-East, Southern Asia and Africa, General Davis retired from ac-ive duty on 1 February, 1970.

Major General Lucius Theus. Director of Accounting and Finance, Office of the Comptroller of the Air Force, and Commander, Air Force Accounting and Finance Center. In this position, he is responsible for operation of the worldwide Air Force Accounting and Finance Network.

154

General Officers of todays Air Force: Left to Right: Brigadier General Thomas Clifford, Brigadier General Rufus Billups, General Daniel James, Major General Lucius Theus and Brigadier General Earl Brown.

June 9, 1945

	Destroyed	Damaged	Total
Aircraft (aerial)	111	25	136
Aircraft (ground)	150	123	273
Barges and Boats	16	24	40
Box cars, Other Rolling Stock	58	561	619
Buildings & Factories	0	23	23
Gun Emplacements	3	0	3
Destroyers	1	0	1
Horse Drawn Vehicles	15	100	115
Motor Transports	6	81	87
Power Transformers	3	2	5
Locomotives	57	69	126
Radar Installations	1	8	9
Tanks on Flat Cars	0	7	7
Oil and Ammunition Dumps	2	0	2
Total Missions	12th Air Force		1267
Total Missions	15th Air Force		311
Total Sorties	12th Air Force		6381
Total Sorties	15th Air Force		9152
Grand Total Missions			1578
Grand Total Sorties			15533
Total Number of pilots sent overseas			450
Total Number of pilots graduated at Tuskegee			992
Total Killed in Action —			66

COMBAT RECORD OF NEGRO AIRMEN

Awards:

Legion of Merit			1
Silver Star			1
Soldier Medal			2
Purple Heart			8
Distinguished Flying Cross			95
Bronze Star			14
Air Medal and Clusters			744

*Final total of Distinguished Flying Crosses awarded to Negro pilots estimated at: 150

(Record through June 9, 1945)

156

These are Our Finest

Not even the sun was bright that day down in Alabama when a handful of Negro cadets went out to add the highways of the military eagle to the paths of the man of color ... went out to answer their Nation's chimerical question: Can a Negro fly and fight in airplanes?

The sun shines right, when things are bright; when the wind blows strong and free.

The challenge was great and the terms were harsh.

Go down there, black boy ... way down to Alabama. Sweat out your days and sit out your nights. And show me ... black boy ... show me you can fly.

The challenge was met by hearts that were strong. From hamlets, towns and cities ... from States like Oregon, Maine, California and Georgia ... came Jones, Smith, Richards and Washington; in a long steady procession they came to Tuskegee.

The days were long. Hup, hup, hup, ho.

Hold that nose down, Mister. Dammit, get that wing up. Can't you see that horizon, Mister? Quit holding that rudder in turns.

But the journey was swift.

From plane to plane, from light to heavy ... from Stearman to Beetee to Ayetee to Thunderbolt ... from Tuskegee to Italy.

Could a Negro fly military planes? Well, here they were in Italy and there sat their P-40s cooling on the ramp.

Pretty good, black boy, p-r-e-t-t-y g-o-o-d. But wait a minute. That's not all. Can you FIGHT in planes? Will you come scudding home with the first burst of fire? Better take it easy for a while, black boy ... right now, better just fly over yonder and shoot up some trains.

Then Anzio. LSTs rolled up to the beaches and dropped out Americans. The going was rough. Blood everywhere. Enemy planes pounding, strating ... pushing us back. Suddenly, swiftly and surely ... out of nowhere came the friendly whine of P-40s. Down, down, down went Jerry. On the beaches, Americans moved forward and slept peacefully that night.

O tell me, lad, of that day long ago; of the "black boy" from Tuskegee over Anzio.

The rest is a matter of record ... a thrill-packed saga of the men who fought in the skies over Europe to save a seemingly ungrateful Nation.

But these men are not whole . . . not full; the best of them lies buried For were they not given escort by an invincible ghost-like squadron of planes? And where are those who won't come back? Remember "Red" Dawson, "Big" Davis and Sindat-Singh?

> "When shall we three meet again?
> In thunder, lightning or in rain?"

Heroes? Men are heroes . . . these are more than men. They are the valiant, the brave . . . the "black boy" tried and true. They are the exploited, the expendable . . . the birds with clipped wings. They are the noble, the greatest . . . these are our finest.

Hats off to the men who tried. Hats off to the men who cried. Hats off . . . to the men who died.

— JOHN H. YOUNG, III.

Bibliography

1. Detroit Chapter, Tuskegee Airmen, Inc.
2. Bureau of Census.
3. The Putt-Putt Air Force, Department of Transportation FAA, by Patricia Strickland.
4. Time Magazine, 28 Oct. 1944.
5. Negroes & The Air Force 1939-1949, Lawrence J. Pazek, Assistant Professor of Military History, USAF Historical Division.
6. "On Clipped Wings" by Judge William H. Hastie, NAACP, October 1943.
7. The Pittsburgh Courier, Newspaper, various Articles 1941-1947.
8. The Norfolk Journal & Guide Newspaper, various articles 1941-1947.
9. Flying Magazine, June 1942.
10. Tuskegee Airmen, by Charles Francis, Bruce Humphries, publisher, 1957.
11. American Magazine, August 1942, "I Got Wings" by Charles DeBow.
12. Employment of Negro Troops in World War II by Ulysses S. Lee, Office of The Chief of Military History, Washington, D.C., 1966.
13. The Hawks, Christy & Shamburger, Wolverine Press, 1972.
14. Brave Men, by Ernie Pyle, Holt & Co. New York, 1944.
15. New York Daily News, Sept. 30, 1943.
16. A Rising Wind, by Walter White, Doubleday, Doran & Co. Garden City, N.Y. 1944.
17. Falcon Newspaper, article by S/Sgt. Irwin Weir, ASAAC.
18. History of the Mediterranean Allied Air Forces, March 1944.
19. Spookwaffe, by Robert W. Williams, unpublished.
20. XV Fighter Command, One Year Later, by Ernie McDowell.
21. History of the 99th FS, Maxwell Field, Ala.
22. History of the 332nd FG, Maxwell Field, Ala.
23. Hidden History, by Major Alan L. Gropman, as delivered at Tuskegee Airmen Convention Aug. 11, 1973, Wash. D.C.
24. Personal interviews by the men and women who shared in the Tuskegee experience.

The following named persons were instrumental in the production of this book with their financial assistance and faithful dedication to purpose . . . it became a reality.

William Bailey
Henry Bowman
Col. William Campbell
Richard Ceasar D.D.S.
Lt. Col. Robert H. Cobbs
William Cross
Russell Desvigne
Robert Drye
William Ellis
Col. Edward Gleed
Tim Harrison *
Tom Heywood A.I.A.*
Mitchell Higginbotham
Robert Higginbotham M.D.
Col. Louis Hill
Jerry Hodges C.P.A.

Atty. Elbert Hudson
Charles F. Jamerson
Carey Jenkins A.I.A. *
James A. Jones *
Claybourne Lockett *
George B. Matthews
Charles H. Moore M.D.
Larry Pickens
Atty. Calvin Porter
Col. Price D. Rice
Robert A. Rose D.D.S.
Lowell C. Steward
James Sullivan
Moses A. Thornton
Atty. James Tolbert
Edward Woodward

*Deceased